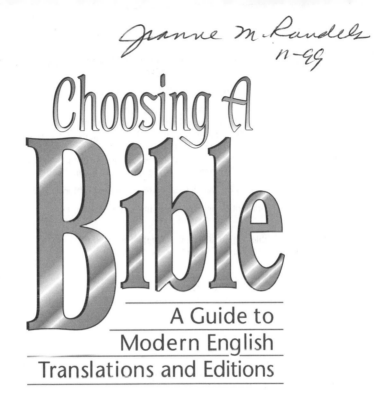

Choosing A Bible

A Guide to Modern English Translations and Editions

Steven M. Sheeley and Robert N. Nash, Jr.

D0061594

Abingdon Press
Nashville

CHOOSING A BIBLE: A GUIDE TO MODERN ENGLISH TRANSLATIONS
AND EDITIONS

Copyright © 1999 by Abingdon Press

This book is printed on recycled, acid-free, elemental-chlorine free paper.

Library of Congress Cataloging-in-Publication Data

Sheeley, Steven M.
   Choosing a Bible: a guide to modern English translations and editions / Steven M. Sheeley and Robert N. Nash, Jr.
      p.   cm.
   Includes index.
   ISBN 0-687-05200-9 (pbk.: alk. paper)
   1. Bible.   English—Versions.   I. Nash, Robert N.   II. Title.
BS455.S53   1999
220.5'2—dc21
                                                                99-16383
                                                                    CIP

99 00 01 02 03 04 05 06 07 08 — 10 9 8 7 6 5 4 3 2 1

MANUFACTURED IN THE UNITED STATES OF AMERICA

Acknowledgments

Collegiality is a wonderful feeling, and we are grateful to have had this second chance to collaborate with each other. Again, we want to thank our families and those churches we call "family" for their unstinting support of our work and our ministry. We also want to thank our students for their questions—and some of their answers—that continue to remind us that learning is an exciting process.

Also invaluable to this project has been our student assistant, Ginny Brewer. Her wit and willingness to take on almost any task make our jobs immeasurably easier.

The Professional Development Committee and Dr. Harold E. Newman, Provost of the College, have again provided financial resources to facilitate the completion of this volume, and we extend to them our fervent thanks for their support.

To all who wonder which Bible will be of most use to them and those they love—we dedicate this book.

Shorter Hill
Rome, Georgia
Lent, 1999

Contents

Introduction

Choosing a Bible today is certainly not easy! The dizzying array of translations and specialty Bibles directed at everyone from athletes to executives to teenagers is both blessing and curse. The good news? There is a Bible for you! The bad news? You'll have to look for it!

How can you make an educated decision when it comes to selecting a Bible? We recommend that anyone who buys a Bible should consider a series of questions before making a selection. In this book we raise these questions and offer suggestions about how you might answer them for yourself. The questions are organized into four groups and will be dealt with in the four chapters that follow.

The first set of questions is primarily historical. How did the Bible come to be in its present form? When was it first translated into English? How can you be sure that the English Bible you hold in your hands is a faithful translation of the text? Chapter 1, "The Making of the English Bible," addresses these questions.

The second set of questions is more theoretical. Why do translations differ? Should you simply trust the translators? Or should you make some effort to understand the processes and philosophies that guided these translations in order to choose one that is suitable for you? What translations are the most important? The most popular? How do translations differ? Chapter 2 contains a short history and evaluation of the major translations available today.

A third set of questions addresses not the translation itself but the form in which you find it. Today every translation is available in more than one format, and so you are confronted with still more choices. What formats exist today? What do you need to consider before you make a selection? Which one best suits your purposes? We take up these questions in chapter 3.

The final set of questions is practical. Now that you know something about the various translations, you must still decide which one to buy. In the final chapter we take up questions about who you, or the reader you are buying for, are and what end you have in mind as you make this purchase.

Why give such thought to choosing a Bible? Because the Bible guides our faith and informs our theology and practice. It is much too important a book to be lifted casually from a bookstore shelf without giving any thought to how it got there in the first place. We have written this book to help you choose an English translation that is most appropriate for you. We hope, in fact, to interest you in the processes of translation and interpretation that have led to the proliferation of versions and formats of the Bible today. The world that the Bible presents to us is both alien and familiar. The type of text you choose to use as a bridge between this day and that time will make a difference in how you understand yourself as a Christian and how you grow in faith. Comparing the insights of scribes, translators, and publishers gives us all a fuller understanding of the Scriptures. So buy a Bible—perhaps more than one—and use it, read it, and let it change you as you hear or hear again the stories of God and of the people of God.

1

The Making of the English Bible

The Bible as we know it today didn't just appear on bookstore shelves complete with leather binding and gold lettering! The journey of the Bible from a collection of ancient tales told by faithful people to the bound volume on the shelf is a fascinating story, full of twists and turns. The word *Bible* comes from the Greek word *biblion,* which means "book" or "papyrus," referring to the plant from which the earliest writing paper was made. The plural form of *biblion* is *biblia,* "books."

Although the Bible is often called "the Holy Book," it is in fact a collection of books written over a period of some 1,100 years. According to the custom of Christians, this collection is divided into two testaments: the Old Testament, which relates the history and faith of Israel, and the New Testament, which contains stories of the life and teachings of Jesus and of the emergence of Christianity.

The Old Testament

The Old Testament emerged out of the oral traditions of the Jewish people, who passed down stories about God's relationship to Israel from generation to generation. These stories were eventually written down and collected. Later they were carefully copied onto scrolls for safekeeping. The oracles of the prophets of Israel and other kinds of history and wisdom literature were added to the collection as well.

Through a lengthy process called canonization, the Jewish people determined which books should be considered sacred and which should not. The word *canon* simply means "an authoritative list for a given community." The books or collections that made the Jewish list of sacred writings were those books to which the faithful turned most often for religious and moral instruction and encouragement. These books were eventually gathered together into a single collection called the Hebrew Scriptures or, for Christians, the Old Testament.

The texts of the Hebrew canon are traditionally divided into three categories: the Law (or Torah), the Prophets, and the Writings. The Torah, which includes the first five books of the Bible (Genesis to Deuteronomy), contains stories of Israel's beginnings. The prophetic literature includes historical books and the oracles of particular prophets of Israel. These books are divided further into two categories, the Former Prophets and the Latter Prophets. The Writings include wisdom literature, proverbs, histories, and other stories, such as Psalms, Ruth, Ecclesiastes, Esther, Daniel, and Chronicles.

The New Testament

The New Testament emerged from the stories about Jesus that his followers told after his death and resurrection. About 45–50 CE, the apostle Paul penned his first letter to the church at Thessalonica. Biblical scholars believe this letter to be the oldest surviving New Testament writing, but there were soon many more.

Toward the end of the second century CE, the Christian church began to make lists of those books that belonged in a *new* testament. Up to this point, the first Christians, like Jesus, knew the Hebrew Scriptures as their Bible. When the canonization process was completed in the fourth century, the New Testament contained the collection with which we are familiar: four Gospels, the Acts of the Apostles, the epistles of Paul, other letters, and the Apocalypse (or Revelation) of John.

Early Translations

Translating Scripture is an ancient art. Both the Old and the New Testaments were translated long ago in order to make them available to wider audiences.

The Septuagint

The Hebrew Scriptures were translated into Greek from Hebrew and Aramaic in the third century BCE. This translation, known as the Septuagint, was intended for Jewish audiences outside of Palestine who could not speak Hebrew. Early Christians used this Greek translation of the Hebrew Scriptures as their Bible.

The Vulgate

The entire Bible was translated into Latin from the original languages in the late fourth and early fifth centuries CE by Jerome, a native of Italy and a high church official. It was officially commissioned by the Bishop of Rome and, because Latin was the language of the common (or "vulgar") people, became known as the Vulgate.

The Three Canons

Slight differences exist between the canons of Judaism, Roman Catholicism, and Protestantism. The Jewish canon includes twenty-four books containing the same texts as the thirty-nine books of the Protestant Old Testament. The Jewish canon divides the books differently, based not on authorial identity but by the amount of text that could fit on one scroll. First and Second Samuel, 1–2 Kings, and 1–2 Chronicles are each considered one book. Likewise Ezra and Nehemiah are combined. So, too, the twelve Minor Prophets appear as one unit.

The Roman Catholic canon consists of the thirty-nine books of the Protestant Old Testament, the twenty-seven books of the New Testament, and seven additional books from the Apocrypha, writings not found in the Hebrew Scriptures. These additional books include Tobit, Judith, the Wisdom of Solomon, Ecclesiasticus, Baruch, 1–2 Maccabees, and additions to Esther and Daniel. They are considered part of the Old Testament, which contains forty-six books in Roman Catholic Bibles.

The Protestant canon recognizes only the thirty-nine books of the Old Testament found in the Hebrew Scriptures and the twenty-seven books of the New Testament.

The History of the English Bible

Jerome's Vulgate served as the official Bible of the church for almost 1,000 years, even after classical Latin ceased to be a spoken language. In time only educated clergy could read it. The Bible was no longer the possession of ordinary Christians. Some recognized this as a dangerous trend in the church. In the late Middle Ages reformers in various countries began to translate the Scriptures into the languages people spoke in their daily lives.

John Wycliffe, an English priest and church reformer of the fourteenth century, is responsible for the first full translation of the Bible from Latin into English. Church authorities condemned the Wycliffe Bible in 1415, fearing that erroneous interpretations might result if the Bible became available in the popular languages of Europe.

Despite such condemnations the invention of the printing press in 1455 resulted in the spread of common-language translations of the Bible across Europe. Martin Luther, the great Protestant reformer, published a German version of the New Testament in 1522; the complete Bible appeared in 1534. Luther's passion for reform was rooted in his contention that the church must return to its original source of authority. In other words, he suggested that Christians should look behind traditions of interpretation, doctrine, and worship to the Scriptures themselves. To this end he translated not from Latin but from the original Greek, Hebrew, and Aramaic manuscripts.

William Tyndale followed Luther's lead in 1525 with an English version of the New Testament translated from Greek. Tyndale fled to Germany to publish his New Testament when authorities in England forbade publication there. He later translated the first five books of the Old Testament and Jonah as well.

In 1535 Tyndale was arrested near Brussels. Convicted of treason for ignoring the prohibitions against common language translations, he was executed in 1536. His followers translated other portions of the Old Testament shortly after his death. Nearly every English translation for the next 200 years borrowed from Tyndale's work.

English Translations in the Sixteenth and Seventeenth Centuries

For most of the sixteenth century England was embroiled in a crisis over the religious direction of the nation. The throne passed back and forth between Protestant and Roman Catholic monarchs; first Catholics and then Protestants were forced to flee to the European continent. Both groups undertook new translations of the Bible to bolster their theological claims.

Tydale's student Myles Coverdale published an English translation drawing on the Vulgate and on Luther's German Bible in 1535. *The Coverdale Bible* received a royal license from King Henry VIII as a part of his challenge to papal authority and was widely disseminated across England.

John Rogers, another of Tyndale's followers, published *Matthew's Bible* in 1537, using the pseudonym Thomas Matthew. Essentially, Rogers added to Tyndale's version his own translation of the Old Testament books Tyndale had not been able to translate before his execution.

When Roman Catholic loyalists regained the ascendency, concerns quickly arose about the heavily Protestant flavor of both the *Coverdale Bible* and *Matthew's Bible*. In 1538, to correct the bias, Thomas Cromwell, an adviser to Henry VIII, called for a new translation. Myles Coverdale revised *Matthew's Bible* in 1539 and republished it as *The Great Bible*. Copies were placed in every church in England.

New versions were required by subsequent reversals of fortune in the English church and state. William Whittingham's *The Geneva Bible* (1560) was popular in Elizabethan England because of its obvious Protestant leanings. But in 1568 *The Bishop's Bible* was published by church leaders who could not tolerate the *Geneva Bible's* intense Calvinist leanings. In exile in France, English Catholics required a new translation. Gregory Martin and others completed a full translation of the Vulgate, publishing the New Testament at Rheims in 1582 and the Old Testament at Douai in 1609–10. Revised by Richard Challoner in 1749, the *Douai-Rheims Bible* served as the official English Bible of Roman Catholics until Ronald A. Knox's version of the 1940s.

The King James Version (KJV)

Dissatisfaction with the heavily Calvinist leanings of the *Geneva Bible* lasted well into the seventeenth century. In 1604 Puritan clergymen convinced King James I of the need for a new translation free of interpretive marginal notes. James himself had voiced disagreement with the notes in the *Geneva Bible,* which he believed interfered with the notion of the divine right of kings.

While the KJV is not without its weaknesses, the most important of which is its reliance on faulty Greek and Hebrew manuscripts, its influence on English-speaking Christians and even on the English language is hard to exaggerate. The KJV provided a common Bible for English Protestantism well into the twentieth century. We will return to the KJV in the next chapter when we discuss differences between various translations. Now we turn to questions about the process of translation.

Translating the Bible

The first task of the translator is to decide what ancient words to translate. If we possessed the original manuscripts (called autographs), we could know with certainty where to begin the translation process. However, the earliest manuscripts have been lost or destroyed and are no longer available. In their place we have thousands of manuscripts written in different times and places, which offer us many variations in the biblical text.

Textual critics are biblical scholars who intensively study the ancient texts to determine which words ought to have a place in the resulting "final" text. They analyze and categorize the various readings, working with thoroughness and precision. The result is published texts of the Hebrew Bible and Greek New Testament that are generally accepted among scholars. Textual critics fashion texts that are as close to the original biblical texts as possible given the resources available.

Textual criticism is only the first step in the process of translating the Bible into English. A successful modern translation must render these texts in English, bridging the gap between the ancient and the modern worlds. This task raises philosophical questions that must be answered before work can begin.

Modern English translations of the Bible can be differentiated by the methods of translation followed by the scholars who produced each version. *Verbal* translations attempt to reproduce the modern English equivalent of each ancient word. *Dynamic* translations are more concerned to reproduce the ancient thoughts and ideas in their modern equivalents. In such versions the translators render each phrase rather than each word of the ancient text. *Paraphrases* attempt to convey to modern readers the same meaning the ancient text conveyed to ancient readers. The paraphrase usually makes little reference to the ancient texts, beginning instead with an already-established English translation. The resulting version is easy to read but runs the risk of losing its connection with the biblical text.

The categories of verbal translation, dynamic translation, and paraphrase are not absolute. Even in strict verbal translations particular phrasings in ancient languages need to be reordered to make sense in English. So verbal translations have more or less dynamism. Some dynamic translations are quite faithful to the ancient texts on which they are based. Others take more liberties, tending toward paraphrase. Figure 1 (p. 17) identifies a few of the major translations on a spectrum that stretches between the pole of a literal word-for-word translation, an impractical reality since it would result in choppy and confusing English, and absolute retellings that would be hard to recognize as our common scriptural heritage. The translations mentioned, along with many other versions, will be discussed in further detail in the next chapter. They are used here simply to orient you to the number of ways in which translators have attempted to communicate faithfully the biblical stories in English.

The Bible demands that its readers come to its pages with the best preparation possible. We hope that this brief discussion of the Bible's history, the development of the canon, textual criticism, and translation philosophy will enable you to be a more discerning and better-prepared reader of the Bible. And with that we turn to the main task of this book: the analysis and evaluation of modern English translations of the Bible.

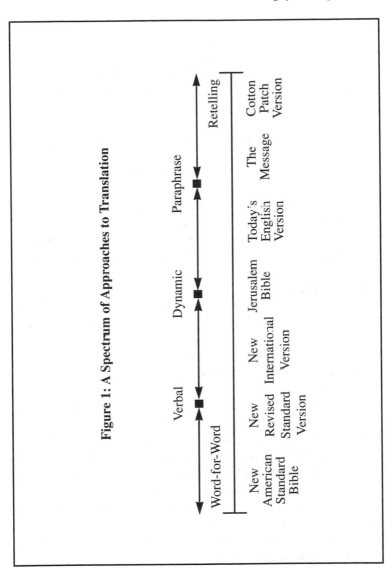

Figure 1: A Spectrum of Approaches to Translation

Word-for-Word

Verbal

Dynamic

Paraphrase

Retelling

New American Standard Bible

New Revised Standard Version

New International Version

Jerusalem Bible

Today's English Version

The Message

Cotton Patch Version

2

Modern Translations:
Verbal, Dynamic, and Paraphrase

It has happened to many of us. You were asked to read a passage of Scripture in Sunday school or worship. After you finished someone asked what translation you had read from, because your Bible didn't say the same thing his or hers did. Many churches have tried to avoid this problem by purchasing pew Bibles, but members who bring their own Bibles may still notice differences between what they read and what they hear. Discovering the differences between translations seldom causes a crisis, but often it leaves someone wondering if his or her Bible is accurate and dependable.

A few years ago such questions rarely arose, for every member of the congregation held the King James Version. The variety of Bible translations present in any congregation on a given Sunday morning these days would astonish churchgoers of the 1940s and 1950s. We have grown accustomed to a variety of translations and almost expect our pastors or Sunday school teachers to read from a version that differs from our own.

This chapter is devoted to a conversation about various English translations of the Bible. Space considerations do not allow us to address every available translation. Consequently, we have chosen to discuss only the most popular and widely available versions, with the exception of a few lesser-known works that are particularly important to the enterprise of translation. We address, in turn, examples of the three approaches to translation introduced in the preceding chapter: verbal, dynamic, and paraphrase. For each translation we provide a summary of the history of its creation and a brief discussion of its strengths and weaknesses. Our conviction that no particular translation is best and that a translation's strengths are often the source of its weaknesses as well will be evident throughout.

Verbal Translations

Verbal translations attempt to translate the Bible into modern English while remaining as close to the grammar, words, rhythm, and order of the ancient languages as possible. We discuss below the parent of all modern English Bibles, the King James Version, and its most important descendants.

King James Version (KJV)

For over 300 years the KJV has been *the* Bible of the English-speaking church. Even though recent modern translations have gained in popularity at the expense of the KJV, it remains the standard by which all new translations are measured. The KJV's impact on English-speaking Christians is immense. Long after we have abandoned the "thee" and "thou" of our Puritan forebears, we continue to use such language to address God. Even the words of Scripture we have committed to memory are more often than not the words of the KJV.

To many people the KJV *is* God's inspired word, and they will defend its honor to the bitter end. Unfortunately, many of these defenders are unaware of the history of the KJV or of the changes that have been made to the version over time.

In chapter 1 we summarized the events that led King James I of England to convene the group that produced the new translation. King James chose the leading biblical scholars of the day to participate and mandated that *The Bishops' Bible* and the original Hebrew and Greek texts serve as the basis of the translation. Marginal notes, which in other versions of the time tended to offend one group or another within the English church, were to be used only to explain Hebrew and Greek words or to point out parallel passages. Distinctive type set off words that had been added to complete a thought, and chapter and verse divisions remained the same. The KJV was published in its entirety in 1611 and went through many editions in the next few years, most of which included changes in the text.

The great strength of this translation lies in the richness of its English. This is especially true in the Bible's many poetic passages. The psalms in the KJV, for example, capture uniquely the vitality and energy of these prayers. Its attention to the way the language sounds when read aloud has much to do with the KJV's popularity and influence.

In addition, the translators of the KJV must be given considerable credit for producing an excellent translation within their context. All translators work within the realities of the texts available, their knowledge of ancient languages, and the limits of modern language to express ancient ideas. The limitations of the KJV are those of history and language rather than of the translators' skill and biblical understanding.

But the KJV "as an English translation for our time" has significant limitations, two of which strike at the heart of the translation, since they have to do with the languages in question: Hebrew, Greek, and English. A translation for some Hebrew words could only be conjectured in 1611 because their appearance in the biblical text was the only example of their usage available. After discoveries of additional Hebrew manuscripts, most notably the Dead Sea Scrolls in the twentieth century, other examples became available, clarifying the meaning of some words. In the same way subsequent discoveries of additional ancient Greek manuscripts have allowed for more accurate translations of New Testament texts. The translators of the KJV simply did not have such information available to them.

A similar limitation of the translation results from changes in the English language over the past 300 years. Some of the words commonly used in the seventeenth century are no longer in use today, and other words have taken on completely different meanings. As with any living language, words are added, taken away, or changed. In short, the modern English language is no longer that of King James's England.

The critical limitation, however, lies in the texts used by the KJV translators. In chapter 1 we mentioned textual criticism, that process by which one arrives at the text to be translated. Two basic theories of textual criticism conflict. The first assumes that the most correct reading is the one that appears in the most manuscripts; in other words, the *majority* rules. Doing textual criticism with this philosophy involves counting manuscript readings and determining a "winner."

The other theory, accepted widely among New Testament scholars today, argues that every manuscript descends from an earlier one from which it was copied; eventually every manuscript can be traced to an original that, unfortunately, no longer exists. The descendants of each original are categorized into "families." Older families are thought to be more authentic than younger ones. The manuscripts from these families carry more *weight* than others when choosing a particular reading from several choices.

The discipline of textual criticism was a fledgling one in the seventeenth century, and many Greek manuscripts that belong to earlier families were discovered buried in the sands of Egypt long after the translators of the KJV were dead. The KJV scholars followed the first theory of textual criticism, basing their work on the words they found in the majority of the manuscripts available to them. Unfortunately, in many places they used texts that subsequent discoveries have proved to be incorrect.

Such questions raise serious concerns about the KJV. These concerns are not serious enough to suggest that the KJV ought to be placed carefully on the shelf or in a museum as an artifact of a particular time and place in Christian history. They are serious enough, though, to suggest that the KJV ought not to be the only translation of the Scriptures used by a Christian. At the very least, such questions about the KJV opened the door for modern translations to challenge its dominance in the life of the church.

Revised Standard Version (RSV)

In twentieth-century North America the RSV was the first such challenger. For almost one hundred years church leaders and biblical scholars had sensed that changes in English usage were diminishing the effectiveness of the King James Version. For this reason the Church of England commissioned a major revision of the King James Version in the 1880s. The Revised Version was the result. An "Americanization" of that revision appeared in 1901, known as the American Standard Version. These revisions remained faithful to the text and language of the King James Version.

Because of disputes over differences between the Revised Version and the American Standard Version, the International Council of Religious Education formed a committee to study the need for further revisions. A committee of thirty-two scholars, representing many Protestant denominations in North America as well as twenty seminaries and colleges, began the translation in 1937. The New Testament was published in 1946. The New and Old Testaments of the RSV were "authorized by a vote of the National Council of Churches of Christ in the U.S.A" and were published together in 1952. An RSV translation of the Apocrypha appeared in 1957.

The most noticeable difference between the King James Version and the RSV is the modernization of the English. Gone are many of the Elizabethan word endings; "sendeth" became "sends," "goeth" became "go," and "saith" became "said." Also absent is the familiar "And it came to pass," often replaced by the more simple "After these things." Another change lies in the words used for direct address. Except when addressing God or the risen Christ, "thee" and "thou" were replaced by "you."

Other changes involved stylistic considerations. Unlike earlier translations, the RSV printed poetic passages of the Old Testament as verse rather than in paragraph form. Quotation marks were added representing the translators' decisions about when discourse ends and narrative begins. The translators also decided to return to the practice of the King James Version of using many different synonyms to translate one Hebrew or Greek word, reversing the practice of the Revised Version and the American Standard Version. Another reversal involved the decision to use "the Lord" in translating the divine name, as the Revised Version and the King James Version had done, rather than using "Jehovah" as the American Standard Version team had done.

The less obvious, but more profound, difference between the King James Version and the RSV, however, results from changes in the Hebrew and Greek texts used for the translation. Using modern textual criticism and taking advantage of recent manuscript discoveries, translators of both the original RSV and its revision in 1971 often chose to use a different text than that used by the translators of the King James Version. In the original version the translators omitted the longer ending of Mark (16:9-20) and the story of the woman caught in adultery (John 7:53-8:11) as inauthentic. Because of the strong reaction to these omissions, most later editions of the RSV restored these passages, along with marginal notes indicating that the passages are not in the most ancient manuscripts.

The RSV received mixed reviews. Many people approved of the attempt to use modern English without ignoring the literary quality found in the Tyndale/King James Version tradition. Some people thought the new translation far too conservative in modernizing the language. By far the most vocal critics, though, were those who considered the RSV to be almost sacrilegious in its attempt to supplant the King James Version. Some attacked the theological bias of the RSV, most notably its tendency to translate passages in the Old Testament prophets in a way that seemed to obscure their obvious reference to Jesus.

In spite of its critics the RSV quietly took its place as one of the dominant English translations of the Bible. A number of commentaries are based on the RSV. Many churches and seminaries chose the RSV as their more-or-less official translation. More than likely this was because it closely follows the best versions of the ancient texts available and the translation committee was broadly representative. In addition, unlike the King James Version, the process of producing the RSV included provisions for ongoing revision, provisions that have allowed the RSV to be revised as changes in usage occur and as new textual discoveries are made.

The RSV is readable and comfortable to many English-speaking Christians, Protestants and Roman Catholics alike. The language is modern enough that it no longer sounds strange to ears used to late twentieth-century English; however, the words and rhythms are not so different from those of the King James Version that they jar ears accustomed to the older version. The credentials of the scholars involved in all phases of the project are also impeccable.

The RSV has its weaknesses, though. The decision to use a number of synonyms for the same Hebrew or Greek word makes it more difficult to trace rhetorical devices such as repetition and wordplays common to ancient writers. A similar problem results from the decision to modernize the words used for direct address. Modern English does not distinguish between the plural and the singular "you." The reader often has no way of knowing if a biblical text addresses a group of people or an individual. Our tendency toward individualism obscures the reality that biblical writers and readers rarely thought of themselves as individuals. Thus a great many of the biblical "you's" are plural.

In general, though, the RSV achieved its stated aims. Squarely in the tradition of the King James Version, it is theologically and textually sound and accessible to the modern reader.

The New American Standard Bible (NASB)

The American Standard Version has other offspring besides the Revised Standard Version. The American Standard Version reflected the state of North American biblical scholarship in the latter half of the nineteenth century; but by the middle of the twentieth century, its language sounded stilted and archaic. As a result the Lockman Foundation, a California not-for-profit corporation dedicated to Christian education, evangelism, and Bible translation, sponsored a new translation. They intended to carry on the legacy of the American Standard Version, translating the Scriptures with accuracy and fidelity to the original languages in both meaning and word order while still producing a more modern translation. This translation, the New American Standard Bible, was to be suitable for serious Bible study as well as for public and private reading. It uses the best Hebrew and Greek texts available and modernizes the archaic language of the American Standard Version. The NASB New Testament was published in stages from 1960 to 1963; the entire Bible followed in 1971.

The NASB is a conservative translation in almost every sense of the word. It is the most thorough attempt to produce a verbal equivalence translation of the ancient biblical texts, reproducing Hebrew and Greek tenses, meanings, and word order with fidelity whenever possible. The NASB is also conservative in its refusal to abandon traditional readings in light of textual evidence that supports a different reading. Examples of this conservative tendency may be found in the NASB's handling of Mark's ending (16:9-20/16:9) and the story of Jesus and the adulterous woman (John 7:53–8:11). These questionable passages are printed in the body of the text, devoid of almost any mark to distinguish them as problematic.

The NASB is as close to a word-for-word translation as we have. Because of this, it is particularly useful for serious Bible study. Its attention to word order and basic meaning makes it a great help to the person translating the Hebrew of the Old Testament or the Greek of the New Testament. But this greatest strength of the NASB is also its greatest weakness. In giving almost slavish attention to the word order and basic meaning of the ancient texts, this version offers a translation that is often stilted and unsuitable for public reading. In English, word order often determines a sentence's meaning. In contrast, Greek and Hebrew can invert or rearrange word order for emphasis without changing the meaning of the sentence. Translating the ancient languages in their word order runs the risk of confusion at best and may even distort the meaning of the passage. In addition, unlike its more "dynamic" cousins, the NASB sometimes misses the meaning of idiomatic expressions in the ancient languages.

In 1995 the Lockman Foundation published The New American

Standard Bible, Updated Edition (NASB Update), to address some of the critical responses to the NASB. In the NASB Update they removed the words "thee" and "thou" and consulted the newest scholarly editions of the Hebrew, Aramaic, and Greek texts. While still committed to preserving the word order of the ancient texts, some concession was made to order the words according to common English usage. The NASB Update's cross-references and grammatical notes are the best and most useful provided by any version.

Just as the NASB Update takes advantages of the strengths of the NASB, however, so also it displays similar weaknesses. Section headings intended to allow the reader an immediate grasp of the syntactical structure of the passage fail because, like the NASB, the NASB Update is intentionally as literal as possible and, therefore, obscures syntactical units. On balance, though, the NASB Update is a step in the right direction. Although still not very suitable for public reading, it is certainly more fluid than the NASB.

The New International Version (NIV)

One of the more popular twentieth-century versions of the Bible is the NIV. By the time the entire Bible was published in 1978, it had advance sales of over one million copies. This new translation was undertaken by leaders of the evangelical Christian community who were dissatisfied with the Revised Standard Version. In 1965 a group of scholars met to make plans for a new, more conservative translation. In 1967 the New York Bible Society (now the International Bible Society) offered to underwrite the cost. Scholars from all over the English-speaking world came together over the next decade to produce this new translation, which has been widely accepted and praised for its scholarship and readability.

Each participant was required to indicate adherence to a written statement reflecting a high view of biblical authority. That all of those who participated in the project were publically committed to the authority of the Bible as God's Word has given this version a reputation as *the* modern translation for conservative/evangelical Christians.

The NIV offers a good compromise between the major verbal translations—namely, the King James Version and the Revised Standard Version—and newer dynamic translations such as Today's English Version and The Living Bible. The NIV was an entirely new translation made by reputable scholars. It also managed to capture a modern style without leaving the style and rhythm of the King James Version too far behind. The NIV translators were a bit eclectic in some of their translation choices, especially in determining the ancient text on which the version is based. At its heart, though, the NIV is a verbal translation that seeks more often than not to remain true to the words and order of the ancient texts. Most discrepancies result from the translators' attempt to produce a conservative translation.

The great strength of the NIV is its readability. It is probably the modern counterpart to the King James Version in terms of the quality of its prose for public reading. It sounds biblical and modern at the same time. The NIV committees are to be commended for their fidelity to the ancient texts and for their sensitivity to modern expression.

Another strength of the NIV lies in its availability and usefulness in a number of different forms. The many formats in which it appears are attractive and inviting; Zondervan was one of the first publishers to make use of technological advances and marketing strategies to offer the NIV in formats that almost everyone could use.

These strengths, however, also contribute to this version's weaknesses. The primary weakness is that in order to make the version readable the NIV translators often chose phrases too colloquial for the standards established for verbal translation. For instance, the powerful Old Testament formula "Thus says/saith Yahweh/the LORD" is rendered as the rather insipid "This is what the LORD says." At other times the same impulse to provide familiar language results in translations that are far too interpretative in nature. One striking example is the NIV's tendency to translate the word *flesh* in the New Testament as "sinful nature," "human nature," and "human" (among others). Such ideas may be present in Paul's use of "flesh," but often Paul means to evoke the *range* of meanings that are part of the word *flesh*.

The "dynamic" nature of the NIV causes another problem for serious Bible study. One of the characteristics of American English is its tendency to avoid repeating the same word within a range of paragraphs or pages. Ancient Hebrew and Greek, as primarily oral languages, used repetition in order to help the hearer or reader understand and remember the story or argument. Recognizing such repetition is often an important part of interpreting biblical passages. Unfortunately, the NIV has followed our modern preferences and used different words (synonyms) to translate the repeated word.

Two more weaknesses should be noted. Again, they are integrally related to what makes this a very strong and useful translation. We refer here to the stated philosophy of the translation project to produce a "conservative/evangelical" translation and the wedding of this philosophy to a marketing strategy. Careful comparison of this translation with other modern verbal translations suggests that, for the most part, the NIV is neither more nor less conservative than the others. The NIV does, however, offer translations that support the interpretations of conservative Christians in passages that have been the subject of controversy. For example, in Isaiah 7:14 the NIV preserves the translation "virgin" rather than "young woman." In other places in the Old Testament, though, this same word is translated in the NIV as "young woman."

The conservative nature of the translation may also be seen in the notes. In the first place, a decision was made to include as few notes as possible in order to avoid confusing the reader. Many significant textual questions are ignored in the notes, giving the reader no indication of textual problems in the translation. Second, many of the notes that are provided follow conservative interpretations solely.

Despite our criticisms, we believe the NIV is a good translation.

Like any translation of the Bible, however, the NIV should not be considered the only true translation. Its great achievement lies in its readability. No other modern English translation has reached the same level and still maintained such a close connection to the ancient languages.

The New International Reader's Version (NIrV) is an edition of the NIV designed to make the Bible accessible to the large number of people in the United States who read below the fourth-grade level. Sentences have been shortened and simplified, and difficult words have been replaced with simpler terms. This version is aimed at children under the age of eight, adults who read at or below the fourth-grade level, and the growing number of people in the United States for whom English is a second language. In addition, it contains a dictionary and numerous helps designed to ease the inexperienced reader into the process of reading the Bible. The NIrV is designed to make the Bible easily accessible to less skilled readers as a beginning step. The ads suggest that after one is introduced to the Bible through the NIrV, one can step up to the NIV.

The New American Bible (NAB)

In 1943 Pope Pius XII changed the face of Roman Catholic biblical scholarship and translation. His encyclical on Scripture studies, *Divino afflante Spiritu,* encouraged Roman Catholic biblical scholars to turn their attention to the ancient biblical languages. In response, North American Roman Catholic bishops called for a new translation of the ancient texts into English for individual study and for worship. An Old Testament was ready by 1969, and the entire Bible was published in 1970.

The translators working on this original edition of the NAB followed a translation philosophy of dynamic equivalence. The reason for its inclusion here is that the revision of the NAB-NT, published in 1986 to replace the 1970 New Testament, follows a verbal translation philosophy. A similar revision is in process for the NAB-OT.

Like most of the translations produced in the last fifty years, the

29

NAB made use of standard critical texts of the Old and New Testaments. Some scholars have disagreed with the committee's choice of texts in certain Old Testament passages, but most of the NAB-OT has been translated from texts that are acceptable in scholarly circles.

That this is a translation specifically aimed at the Roman Catholic community in the United States has left the NAB open to suspicions of theological bias; however, the NAB remains a good modern translation. A few readings and notes do mark the Roman Catholic loyalties of this version. As expected, the woman in Isaiah 7:14 is a "virgin." References to "brothers" of Jesus remain in the New Testament, but footnotes inform us that the Greek word used in the ancient world often refers to any kind of relative, not necessarily to siblings. At the same time, the note on Mark 6:3 indicates that it is only the church's doctrine of the perpetual virginity of Mary that raises any interpretative doubts about the nature of Jesus' siblings at all.

The NAB is the product of a thoughtful and careful translation process. It is useful not only for devout American Catholics, but also for those Protestants who desire more understanding of Roman Catholic biblical scholarship. In fact, the loudest critics have not been Protestants, but Catholics who object to the gender-inclusive language of the translation. The forms of the ancient languages rarely leave doubt as to the gender of the word in question, but some words have a different gender reference in English than they possessed in the ancient languages. The process of translation always involves interpretation and paraphrase, even in those translations that attempt to maintain as close a connection as possible to the ancient languages. The NAB represents a genuine, but cautious, attempt to be gender-inclusive in its language.

The New King James Version (NKJV)

In 1982 Thomas Nelson Publishers produced the NKJV, a new translation from the Hebrew and Greek texts. This translation was designed to recapture that part of the Bible market that was no longer comfortable with the language of the seventeenth century but didn't want to give up the King James Version.

The claims of the NKJV were high: to maintain the order, power, and grace of the King James Version; to maintain the same fidelity to the ancient texts and attention to public readability; and to modernize the language of the translation but still retain the familiar phrasing and rhythm of the King James Version. It would be new, but not *too* new.

Unfortunately, the NKJV does not address the major weakness of the King James Version: its flawed original language text. The King James Version translators had little choice but to use the majority or "received" text in 1611; most of the earlier manuscripts lay as yet undiscovered. Given their academic excellence and deep reverence for the Bible, one would suppose that the translators of the NKJV would use the best manuscript available, no matter what difficulties it posed. Reverence for the text in the NKJV, however, seems to be more for the language of the King James Version than for the ancient texts of the Bible.

The translation does little more than update the language of the King James Version. Archaic forms ("thee" and "thou," "sayeth" and "sayest") have been eliminated in favor of more modern speech patterns. Places where the King James Version is known to be inaccurate in its grammar and idiom have been corrected and smoothed over to conform to modern usage. However, the NKJV has been criticized for producing a language never used by any generation of English-speaking people. It is a curious combination of the new and the old, a new patch on an old garment.

The NKJV has not succeeded either in supplanting the King James Version or in taking much away from the other modern English translations.

The 21st Century King James Version (KJ21)

Convinced that the scholarship and literary artistry of the translators of the King James Version remain unmatched, William D. Prindle formed a publishing company whose primary purpose was to produce, market, and distribute a modern version of the 1611 masterpiece. The KJ21, published in 1994, was created by filtering the King James Version through *Webster's New International Dictionary, Second Edition, Unabridged.* If Webster considered a word to be archaic or offered a more clear and modern synonym, the word was changed. In this way none of the majesty and artistry of the King James Version was lost, but the translation became significantly clearer to modern readers.

Without apology or pretense, Prindle and his publishing company built their version on the foundation of the King James Version. Prindle is aware of the textual controversies but believes that the benefits of remaining firmly in the King James Version tradition far outweigh the problems.

A second problem is stylistic. Prindle distinguishes between certain types of biblical texts by using different typefaces. While this may sound like a helpful tool, it implies graphically that some portions of the text are more important than others. In fact, those passages that are "less familiar, less frequently quoted and memorized, and less frequently included in lectionaries and for sermon texts, but which are of specific interest to Bible scholars, historians, and social scientists" are printed in the smallest type. The message that these verses are insignificant is clear.

Finally, those who market the KJ21 seem prone to exaggeration. Claims that the KJ21 rescues the Bible from the ravages of "modern liberal" scholars are more polemical than substantive.

On a positive note, however, Prindle is honest about his unusual method of modernization and its limitations. One can applaud his diligence, even if one disagrees with his starting point. Prindle is now in the process of working on what will be entitled The Third Millennium Bible, which will add a modernized Apocrypha to the KJ21.

The New Jerusalem Bible (NJB)

While the Jerusalem Bible (JB), which was published in 1966, followed a dynamic translation philosophy, its revision, the NJB, moved to the verbal side of the spectrum. The NJB was published in

1985, and a Reader's Edition followed in 1989. The Jerusalem Bible and the NJB provide more scholarly aids than does the other modern Roman Catholic translation, the New American Bible. The Jerusalem Bible and the NJB include well-written introductions to sections of the Bible, helpful introductions to each book, and explanatory notes.

The NJB was a substantial improvement over the Jerusalem Bible, which was based on a French translation, *La Bible de Jérusalem.* The translators of the NJB made a point of working directly from the ancient texts, using the French version only when the words of the ancient manuscripts were not clear. In addition, the Jerusalem Bible followed a dynamic philosophy of translation. Although sometimes resulting in magnificent prose, it was often criticized for interpreting rather than translating the biblical text. The NJB, a verbal translation, has avoided these problems.

As a study Bible the overwhelming strength of the NJB remains its introductory and explanatory material, examples of some of the finest Roman Catholic biblical scholarship. It is balanced in its approach, and it takes full advantage of the scholarly work on the Bible done during the last two centuries. Like the New American Bible, the NJB is designed for a Roman Catholic audience. It contains the entire range of books considered canonical by the Roman Catholic communion, including those of the Apocrypha, and has printed them in canonical order.

Interestingly, the NJB gives significant attention to problematic passages that raise questions about church doctrine. For instance, in Isaiah 7:14 the NJB chooses to translate the Hebrew as "young woman," rather than to follow the Greek (Septuagint) translation of "virgin." The NJB does, though, provide an excellent note explaining the choice of the Septuagint and the resulting Jewish tradition, which the Gospel of Matthew picks up and quotes as a prophecy of the virginal conception of Jesus. Unlike the New American Bible, the NJB chooses not to tread carefully around references in the Gospels to brothers and sisters of Jesus. A note to Matthew 12:46 points out that the Greek word "brother" may also mean close relative, but neither the translation nor its notes lays out or defend the doctrine of the perpetual virginity of Mary.

The weaknesses of the NJB are quite similar to those of the New International Version. While less dynamic than the Jerusalem Bible, the NJB still tends to consider fidelity to the modern expression of English more important than fidelity to the ancient manuscripts. In other words, the NJB displays a tendency to interpret rather than to translate. For instance, if a more literal translation of Paul's Greek does not permit a smoothly flowing and readily understood English passage, the NJB, like the New International Version, tends to rearrange Paul's language and clarify it, at once changing and narrowing Paul's meaning.

Like many other modern English translations, the NJB has made a conscious attempt to be inclusive in its language. It is perhaps the most conservative translation in this regard, choosing not to address the question of gender-inclusive references to God or even to find a new word with which to translate the Greek *adelphos* (brother). That the translators of the NJB were aware of the need to pay careful attention to the gender bias of both the ancient and the modern languages, though, adds another voice to the growing call for sensitivity and thoughtfulness in translating the Bible.

The NJB retains more of the rhythm and structure of the ancient languages than does the Jerusalem Bible, particularly in the Old Testament, while continuing to attend to the literary and stylistic flow of the translation. This makes the NJB more suitable than the Jerusalem Bible for public reading and worship. The reader will often find this version to be refreshingly different; but in light of its interpretative tendencies, it ought to be read alongside other translations.

The New Revised Standard Version (NRSV)

As its name suggests, the NRSV descends directly from the King James Version through the Revised Standard Version. Like many of the other verbal translations discussed in this chapter, the creation of the NRSV was guided by two main principles: fidelity to the ancient biblical languages and reverence for the literary and formal tradition begun by the King James Version. In addition, a series of scholarly and textual discoveries, which had an impact on the texts underlying the Old Testament of the Revised Standard Version, and further changes in the English language and in American culture necessitated a revision. In terms of language, expressions and idioms used in the 1950s no longer had the same meaning twenty years later. In addition, many people in the church had raised questions about the exclusiveness of the Bible's language, particularly in passages where the ancient texts used words that were inclusive in nature. These concerns, philosophical as well as cultural, prompted the Policies Committee of the Revised Standard Version (a part of the National Council of Churches) to commission a new translation. After some fifteen years the NRSV was published in 1989.

Like its predecessor, the NRSV is a translation based on the most accepted scholarly versions of the ancient texts. In fact, because the translation committee of the NRSV shared some members with the committee working on a new edition of the Greek New Testament, the NRSV translators even had access to any changes that might be made in the latter. Like those who worked on the Revised Standard Version, the NRSV translators were concerned to produce a version that would be suitable both for serious Bible study and for proclamation.

For the most part, scholars have considered the NRSV a success. As a recent entry into the marketplace, the NRSV was able to reap the benefits of current biblical scholarship. Demonstrating their high opinion of this version, publishers such as Oxford, Cambridge, and HarperCollins chose the NRSV as the basis of their study editions.

The greatest strength of the NRSV is that it achieves a more modern translation that is somewhat similar to the language of the King James Version while also acceptable to contemporary, and especially North American, readers. It updates the language of the Revised Standard Version while preserving continuity. For example, Psalm 50:9 has been changed from "I will accept no bull from your house" (RSV) to "I will not accept a bull from your house" (NRSV).

The NRSV translators also accepted the challenge to consider issues of gender-inclusive language. Heeding calls from many quarters to recognize and address the power of language to create and maintain unjust relations between groups of people, the NRSV committee was charged with eliminating exclusive language when such elimination did not destroy the meaning of the original languages. Some words in the ancient texts were intended to be gender inclusive; but because the languages had few, if any, words that would make this intention clear, the language was nominally masculine. Such words could easily be translated with more inclusive terms, and they would then reflect more clearly the intention of the text.

For their efforts the translation committee of the NRSV has been rather severely criticized. Some critics have argued that the NRSV goes too far with inclusive language and transgresses the meaning of the text. Others have argued that it does not go nearly far enough; inclusive language is used inconsistently and could have been employed more often. In particular, these latter critics have disagreed with the restriction that inclusive language be used when referring to human beings but not when referring to God. The discussion that followed resulted in the publication of the NRSV in a significantly different format.

In 1995 Oxford University Press unveiled The New Testament and Psalms: An Inclusive Version, a new version of the NRSV that had been edited in order

> to *replace or rephrase all gender-specific language not referring to particular historical individuals, all pejorative references to race, color, or religion, and all identifications of persons by their physical disability alone, by means of paraphrase, alternative renderings, and other acceptable means of conforming the language of the work to an inclusive idea* (pp. viii-ix).

Immediately dubbed the PC (politically correct) Bible, this inclusive version became the focus of reports on CNN and in the *Wall*

Street Journal. It generated considerable publicity that probably aided sales. More important, though, the publicity brought the question of inclusive language back into public debate.

This new version of the NRSV is unlikely to challenge the popularity of other verbal translations. Its attempt to address the issue of inclusive language for God will interest librarians and scholars but is of questionable value for others. Such changes are simply too radical to be accepted by a broad range of Bible readers. In addition, anyone who has tried to use gender-inclusive language in a consistent manner is aware of how difficult and often cumbersome the process becomes. At the root of the problem lies the fact that most languages, including English, use pronouns that possess gender. To be consistently inclusive one must either avoid pronouns or add references to the other gender. Both strategies are awkward. While the idea of God as "Father-Mother" is theologically sound, the phrase will not gain ready acceptance among most churchgoers in the immediate future.

This version goes beyond the debate over gender-inclusive language to address other barriers to full inclusion in the church as well. Citing Luther's translation of the Bible into German as an example of the Bible's power over language, the editors of this volume tried "to *anticipate* developments in the English language with regard to specificity about a number of issues such as gender, race, and physical disability" (p. viii). Therefore, this version refers to "enslaved people," "people with leprosy," and "blind people." Even references to God's "right" hand are translated in terms of power or nearness rather than "right" or "left" so as not to alienate left-handed persons.

It is certainly not our intention to dismiss this version. Its presence bears testimony to the sensitivity with which Christians are beginning to treat each other and those outside the church. But this version's attempt to influence the modern English language rather than to translate the ancient texts faithfully crosses the line from translation into interpretation. It presents the Bible as it *should be,* not as it is.

This inclusive version fills an important niche in the landscape of modern English translations of the Bible. Perhaps it will influence some translators to change their use of language. It may also influence popular perceptions of gender identity as it relates to God. In the meantime, the less inclusive but well-regarded NRSV continues to grow in popularity, especially among scholars.

Dynamic Translations

Given the strength of the King James Version among English-speaking Christians, new translations had a difficult time winning widespread acceptance. Each new version met resistance if it strayed too far from the revered original. Verbal translations, which followed closely the philosophy of the King James Version and often drew heavily on the language of that version as well, were the first to gain credence. However, alongside the development of the verbal translations, other approaches were also being followed. Some scholars, preachers, and evangelists were convinced that the differences between the English language spoken today and that spoken by our ancestors is so great that textual fidelity is less important than rendering the texts in language that sounds familiar to ordinary Christians. These people began to publish translations that sound very modern—and just a little bit strange.

For over one hundred years Bible translators have attempted to provide an easily readable Bible in common, everyday English by the methods of dynamic translation. Dynamic versions differ from verbal translations in that their primary purpose is to express the meaning of the ancient text in fluid modern English rather than by word-for-word fidelity to the original. Dynamic translations are often easily identified either by subtitles that draw attention to the contemporary nature of the version or by catchy titles that appeal to a popular audience.

Early Twentieth-Century Dynamic Translations
A number of dynamic translations were produced in the first half of the twentieth century. The Twentieth Century New Testament was

published in 1901–2. This translation provided a means for native English speakers to "read the most important part of their Bible in that form of their own language which they themselves use." The preface noted that "the English of the Authorized Version (King James) . . . is in many passages difficult, or even quite unintelligible to the modern reader." Interestingly, the translators elected to print the Bible with the books of the New Testament arranged in chronological order.

One of the scholars who served as a consultant to The Twentieth Century New Testament was Richard Francis Weymouth. His own translation appeared in 1903, the year after his death, and was entitled The New Testament in Modern Speech. For the translation Weymouth used his own Greek text, the Resultant Greek New Testament. He also indicated that his purpose was not "to supplant the Versions already in general use" but rather to "furnish a succinct running commentary to be used side by side with its elder compeers."

In 1924 Helen Montgomery published a highly respected translation of the New Testament, The Centenary Translation, in commemoration of the one hundredth anniversary of the American Baptist Publication Society. Montgomery's purpose was to "make a translation chiefly designed for the ordinary reader, intended to remove the veil that a literary or formal translation inevitably puts between the reader of only average education and the meaning of the text."

James Moffatt, a Scottish pastor and biblical scholar and arguably the best-known Bible translator in the first half of the twentieth century, published The New Testament: A New Translation in 1913. A translation of the Old Testament followed in 1924, and a revised edition of the entire Bible appeared in 1935. Moffatt's translation set the standard by which later dynamic versions of the Bible were judged. His purpose was "to convey to the reader something of the direct homely impression made by the original on those for whom it was written." For the first time, modern English speakers heard the Scriptures in the kind of common idiom in which the earliest Greek and Hebrew readers of the Bible heard it. Moffatt did take some liberties with the text. He added culturally specific references such as bag-pipes, which he included among the musical instruments played as people bowed before King Nebuchadnezzar's image (Daniel 3:10), and a linen "kilt" for David to wear as he danced before the ark of the covenant (2 Samuel 6:14). He also transposed whole passages, for example, repositioning John 3:22-30 between 2:12 and 2:13 and completely deleting 1 Timothy 5:23, which says, "take a little wine for the sake of your stomach." All the same, Moffatt's Bible provided a refreshing model for future translations and helped to popularize an idiomatic approach to the translation process.

In 1923 Edward J. Goodspeed produced The New Testament: An American Translation. Four years later, a team headed by J. M. Powis Smith published The Old Testament: An American Transla-tion. In his introduction, Smith wrote that the translation "tries to be American in the sense that the writings of Lincoln, Roosevelt, and Wilson are American. This does not imply any limitation of our mother-tongue, but if anything an enrichment of it." The Goodspeed and Smith translations were combined in The Bible: An American Translation, which appeared in 1931. Then, following Goodspeed's translation of the Apocrypha in 1938, the Old Testament, New Tes-tament, and Apocrypha were brought together in The Complete Bible: An American Translation (1939). This work is considered the American counterpart to Moffatt's British translation.

An excellent Roman Catholic rendering of the New Testament from the Vulgate into English appeared in 1945. Ronald A. Knox, an Anglican convert to Roman Catholicism and retired chaplain of Trin-ity College at Oxford, completed The New Testament in English at the insistence of Roman Catholic officials in England and Wales. Knox published a translation of the Old Testament in 1949 and of the entire Bible in 1955.

Two other dynamic translations deserve brief mention. In his The Complete Bible in Modern English (NT, 1895; entire Bible, 1903), Ferrar Fenton translates Genesis 1:1 as "By Periods GOD created that which produced the Suns; then that which produced the Earth."

Clarence Jordan's editions of The Cotton Patch Version, published in the late 1960s and early 1970s, translated not only the words of the Bible but also its location. Jordan's translations of Paul's epistles, Luke and Acts, Matthew and John (eight chapters only), and the general epistles are set in the American South.

The New Testament in Modern English (Phillips)

In the 1940s J. B. Phillips wrote what has become one of the most popular dynamic English translations of the New Testament in the modern era. While he was ministering to young people in a bombed-out section of London in 1941, it occurred to Phillips that his parishioners might benefit from an easily readable account of the early church's struggle with persecution. He was particularly concerned that "these youngsters, who were by no means unintelligent, simply did not understand Bible language."

After reading Phillips's translation of Colossians in 1943, C. S. Lewis wrote that "it was like seeing a familiar picture after it's been cleaned." This encouragement resulted in Phillips's Letters to Young Churches, a translation of all of Paul's epistles, published in 1947. Phillips added the Gospels (1952), Acts (1955), and Revelation (1957). The entire New Testament was published in 1958, followed by a translation called The Four Prophets (Amos, Hosea, Isaiah 1–35, and Micah) in 1963 and a revision of the New Testament in 1972.

Phillips's translation was well received and quite popular through the 1960s and 1970s for several reasons. It was printed with verse numbers only at the first line of each section, giving it a contemporary look. Section headings helped the reader find familiar passages even without the verse numbers. Most notably, Phillips used literary creativity in shaping the text. He tried "to imagine myself as each of the New Testament authors writing his particular message for the people of today." He hoped that this process would help him to capture Matthew's precision, Mark's bluntness, Luke's sympathetic nature, and John's mysticism. This imaginative approach alone makes his translation valuable.

Several passages in Phillips's 1972 edition achieve his stated goal of bringing clarity to the King James Version text. He translates "my heart's desire" in Romans 10:1 as "from the bottom of my heart." He warms up the King James Version of Romans 13:8 ("Owe no man any thing, but to love one another") with an encouragement to "Keep out of debt altogether, except that perpetual debt of love which we owe one another." His translation of Matthew 5:5 is perhaps the best translation ever of this often misunderstood beatitude: "Happy are those who claim nothing, for the whole earth will belong to them!"

Phillips's translation is a bit puzzling at certain points. Despite his effort to render a smooth reading in English, he occasionally lapses into an awkward literalism. Consider Matthew 8:26 and 14:31, in which the disciples and Peter are referred to as "you little-faiths" and "you little-faith" respectively. At other points the translation becomes a bit too familiar for the context. In Matthew 27:40, as Jesus is crucified, the crowd mocks him with these words: "Hi, you who could pull down the Temple and build it up again in three days—why don't you save yourself?" as if it were the most natural thing in the world to greet a dying man with a cheery "Hi"!

Two other weaknesses are apparent. The translation uses gender exclusive language throughout. Phillips does not even avoid using "men" at points when an appropriately inclusive designation would read smoothly. Also, he sometimes works against his own goal of providing a readable version by choosing difficult English words. Consider the following examples: "palpable frauds" in Titus 1:16, "invidious distinctions" in James 2:9, "slightest prevarication" in 1 Peter 2:22, and "serried ranks of witnesses" in Hebrews 12:1.

Despite these inadequacies, Phillips offers a translation that renders particular passages in a uniquely memorable fashion and that gives equal weight to both the needs of its readers and the concerns of the ancient writers.

The Jerusalem Bible (JB)

In 1966 the JB provided the first opportunity ever for English-speaking Roman Catholics to read an officially sanctioned translation of the Bible from the original languages. Still, as we noted above in introducing the New Jerusalem Bible, the JB is dependent on a French translation of the Bible, *La Bible de Jérusalem.*

The 1966 edition includes the voluminous notes of the one-volume French translation. It also contains a number of helpful tables and maps in the appendixes. In addition, it includes the Apocrypha (Tobith, Judith, 1–2 Maccabees, Wisdom, Ecclesiasticus, and additions to Daniel and Esther) in their original canonical order, not grouped together between the testaments.

This translation goes to great lengths to appeal to readers outside the Roman Catholic faith. In fact, many Protestants are hardly aware of its Catholic flavor. This is especially true of the 1968 Reader's Edition, published in paperback, which is probably the version with which most people are familiar. Perhaps the most helpful feature for Protestant readers of both editions is that biblical names are printed in the form found in the Revised Standard Version. While Roman Catholic doctrinal positions are spelled out in the extensive notes of the 1966 edition, these comments were removed from the Reader's Edition. One Catholic peculiarity that sometimes confounds Protestants is the use of the word *holocaust* in place of "burnt offerings." The JB, however, is a translation that has found an extensive and appreciative audience in Protestant churches.

Such literary luminaries as J. R. R. Tolkien and Robert Speaight had a hand in shaping the English of the JB. The version has been praised for its powerful language and effective storytelling. Its translation of Philippians 2:5-11 is perhaps the best example of this simplicity and literary power:

> His state was divine,
> yet he did not cling
> to his equality with God
> but emptied himself
> to assume the condition of a slave,
> and became as men are;

and being as all men are,
he was humbler yet,
even to accepting death,
death on a cross.
But God raised him high
and gave him the name
which is above all other names
so that *all beings*
in the heavens, on earth and in the underworld,
should bend the knee at the name of Jesus
and that every tongue should acclaim
Jesus Christ as Lord,
to the glory of God the Father.

The JB has been criticized regarding a number of small but significant details. It fails to provide modern equivalents for monetary and weight designations in the ancient world. It alone among all modern translations uses the plural of the word *grace* in 1 Corinthians 1:4: "I never stop thanking God for all the *graces* you have received through Jesus Christ." In a rather glaring oversight, it omits "in one body" from 1 Corinthians 12:13.

Much more traditional in its translation philosophy than is Phillips's version, the JB is dynamic but does not stray far from the ancient texts. For this reason it is probably a more valuable exegetical tool than is Phillips's translation. However, the serious Bible student will want to secure a copy of the original 1966 edition in order to take full advantage of the helpful notes and other supplements.

The New English Bible (NEB)

In October 1946, a conference of representatives from the Church of England, the Church of Scotland, and the Methodist, Baptist, and Congregational churches of Great Britain met in Westminster to consider initiating a new translation of the Bible. They recommended that such a translation be complely new and not merely a revision of the King James Version. Subsequently, a joint committee headed by J. W. Hunkin, Bishop of Truro, and including representatives from many Protestant traditions (and later a few Roman Catholic observers) appointed panels of translators for the Old Testament, the New Testament, and the Apocrypha and a panel for stylistic and literary concerns. The translation team hoped to appeal to people who rarely attended church and were put off by the stately English of the King James Version. They also intended for their version to appeal to young people who wanted a more contemporary translation and to Christians who had become overly familiar with the King James Version. The translation was to be "genuinely English in idiom, such as will not awaken a sense of strangeness or remoteness." It aimed for a "timeless English" that would be neither old-fashioned in tone nor too trendy to survive and that would possess "sufficient dignity to be read aloud."

Under the direction of C. H. Dodd, the panels produced a translation of the New Testament in 1961. Published by the university presses at Oxford and Cambridge, it quickly became a best-seller. Godfrey Driver joined Dodd in leading the translation team in 1965, and the entire Bible was published in 1970. It, too, sold well. Nonetheless, many people were critical of the NEB, which was perceived as being an intentional replacement for the King James Version.

Biblical scholars raised various questions regarding the translation. In several places the NEB translators added short phrases that shade the meaning of the text. These problematic translations include Genesis 1:1, which takes considerable license when it adds the words "of creation" to "In the beginning." John 1:12 is translated "But to all who did receive him, to those who have yielded him their allegiance, he gave the right to become children of God," as if "yielded him their allegiance" and "believed in his name" had the same meaning.

The cultural flavor of the translation is obvious throughout the text, with British spellings and references to British forms of currency. For a translation that set out to use contemporary English, the

NEB is replete with old-style British words. Consider "foregather" (Job 1:4), "panniers" (Job 5:5), "batten" (Proverbs 5:10), and "bedizened" (Revelation 18:17).

The NEB is a text for scholars, particularly those who are attracted by its innovative approach to resolving questions about the Greek text. At the same time, this means that that the NEB should be used with caution. Outside the choice of text, its translation philosophy is traditional enough to warrant use by serious students of the Bible, and the style of its English is formal enough for public reading.

The Revised English Bible (REB)

A revision of the New English Bible was published in 1989 as The Revised English Bible. A number of new member denominations and societies were added to the joint committee, including the Roman Catholic Church, the United Reformed Church, the Moravian Church, and the Salvation Army. REB translators followed much the same process as their New English Bible forebears, dividing into panels to translate the Old Testament, the New Testament, and the Apocrypha respectively. They departed from their predecessors' use of an eclectic Greek text however, preferring the 1979 Nestle-Aland *Novum Testamentum Graece.*

Several quite obvious changes were made in the new edition. God is addressed in the REB with the less formal "you" rather than "thou." Some effort is made to alter the use of gender-exclusive language, though such changes are quite minimal and sporadic for a translation of this period. The translation remains quite free of subheadings, at least when compared to other versions, though the REB panels added a number of new ones. The REB departs from its predecessor with its traditional format, which significantly alters the New English Bible's rather book-like and innovative appearance. Finally, considerable effort was put into reducing the British flavor of the New English Bible.

The REB received extensive accolades for its readability. It effectively modernizes the English of the New English Bible, which was already generally accepted as a translation for public reading. The Beatitudes of Matthew 5 express this significant improvement. Matthew 5:3 changes from "How blest are those who know their need of God" (NEB) to "Blessed are the poor in spirit" (REB). Psalm 23:2 in the REB offers another example of the translation's beauty and readability. "And leads me beside the waters of peace" becomes "he leads me to water where I may rest."

Unfortunately, several awkward translations also reappear in the REB, including Proverbs 19:29 ("There is a rod in pickle for the arrogant") and Song of Songs 1:7 ("that I may not be left picking lice as I sit among your companion's herds"). Neither the New English Bible nor the REB offers much in the way of notes to assist the reader to understand such difficult passages or to explain their use of a verse translation that deviates from more traditional renderings.

The REB has been roundly criticized for its sporadic and quite limited use of gender-inclusive language, especially since one of its stated purposes was to avoid male-oriented language. To their credit, the translators changed "man" in Genesis 1:26 and "mankind" in Genesis 6:1 to "human beings" and "the human race" respectively. But the REB then reverts to male-specific language in passages such as Matthew 4:4 and Luke 4:4 ("Man is not to live on bread alone"), and John 12:25 ("Whoever loves himself is lost, but he who hates himself in this world will be kept safe for eternal life").

The REB stands as a worthy successor to the New English Bible, particularly as a source for scholarly study of the use of texts in Bible translations and as a readable version for use in public worship.

The New Century Version (NCV)

In the 1970s the World Bible Translation Center decided to create a Bible for the hearing impaired. The result was a simple and readable text that led to the translation of the International Children's Bible (ICB), which was a forerunner to the NCV. The New Testament translation of the International Children's Bible was released in 1983, followed by the entire Bible in 1986. A number of guidelines directed the translation effort. The vocabulary, on about a third-grade level, was limited to words in the *Living Word Vocabulary*, a reference guide used in the preparation of *World Book Encyclopedia*. The translators also avoided long sentences, used modern weight designations, and maintained consistent and familiar use of place-names.

Conservative evangelical leaders greeted the International Children's Bible enthusiastically, but representatives of mainline denominations were troubled by the anti-Jewish rhetoric that pervaded the translation. In later revisions some phrases were changed to correct the anti-Jewish flavor.

The success of the International Children's Bible inspired an edition for adults called the New Century Version, published in 1991. A new translation team was appointed, since this new version would have a much different target audience. Among the translators were biblical scholars from across the spectrum of evangelical Protestantism who represented a number of conservative seminaries and colleges.

The translators accepted the restrictions on reading level and vocabulary of the International Children's Bible. They also used modern equivalents for currency, weights, and measures and chose only the most familiar name for a geographical location (e.g., Lake Galilee rather than Lake Gennesaret or Sea of Tiberias). The meanings behind ancient customs were clarified, as were the meanings of words whose usage in English has changed in recent years (e.g., "devote" is rendered "destroyed as an offering to the Lord"). The NCV also made every effort to use gender-inclusive language when such language preserved the original meaning of the text.

The clarity of the NCV as well as its use of gender-inclusive language is evident in its translation of Psalm 8:4: "But why are people important to you? Why do you take care of human beings?" Its rendering of Matthew 4:4 (see also Luke 4:4) is equally refreshing: "A person does not live by eating only bread, but by everything God says." The NCV contains a number of fresh interpretations that rank it among the clearest English translations available today.

The use of a limited vocabulary occasionally detracts from the beauty of the translation. Genesis 1:1 is translated "In the beginning God created the sky and the earth," which does not carry the aesthetic power of the more traditional "heavens." The Beatitudes in Matthew 5 may suffer more than any other passage as a result of this limitation:

> Those people who know they have great spiritual needs are
>   happy, because the kingdom of heaven belongs to them.
> Those who are sad now are happy, because God will comfort them.
> Those who are humble are happy, because the earth will
>   belong to them.

Finally, the effort to create a clear translation is sometimes hindered by improper sentence construction, such as that found in Psalm 23:3*b*: "He leads me on paths that are right for the good of his name."

The NCV is a clear and concise translation that is helpful to both the serious Bible scholar and the devotional reader. It is to be commended for its use of gender-inclusive language despite its predominately male translation team. Unfortunately, it should always be viewed with healthy suspicion by those Christian traditions outside of conservative and Protestant evangelicalism that had no hand in its translation.

New Living Translation (NLT)

In July 1996 a fresh new translation of the Scriptures hit bookstore shelves. With its attractive, contemporary cover, the NLT touts itself as "Easy to Understand" and "Relevant for Today."

The NLT team of some ninety translation specialists aimed to revise and update Kenneth Taylor's popular 1970s Bible paraphrase, The Living Bible, by checking Taylor's work against the ancient languages and fashioning a new dynamic translation of the Bible that would stand on its own. The translation team consisted of scholars from a wide range of conservative and evangelical Protestant traditions. Their mission was to make the NLT "both exegetically accurate and idiomatically powerful."

The NLT translators followed a number of guidelines in the quest for accuracy and readability: Ancient weights and measures were converted to modern North American equivalents. Ancient currency was identified according to its approximate weight in precious metals. Time designations were updated to approximate modern equivalents either by references to seasons or actual dates when possible. Idiomatic expressions were translated into their closest modern English equivalent. Metaphorical language was generally maintained, though an effort was made to help the reader to understand the meaning of the metaphor. For example, the phrase "Your neck is like the tower of David" is translated as "Your neck is as stately as the tower of David" (Song of Songs 4:4). The translation makes every effort to be gender-inclusive.

Several kinds of footnotes are provided to help to clarify the text. These notes identify references to Old Testament passages, cultural and historical information, textual variants, the meaning of proper names, transliterations of place-names, and alternative renderings.

The Tyndale Bible verse finder at the beginning of the volume betrays the conservatism of the editors. The first entry directs the reader to verses that condemn abortion, although no direct reference to such a practice exists in the Bible. Curiously, homosexuality is condemned, but divorce is not even listed.

The NLT is based on The Living Bible, but significant changes have been made throughout the new translation. The most infamous verse in The Living Bible is Saul's curse of Jonathan in 1 Samuel 20:30 ("You son of a bitch!"). The NLT reads, "You stupid son of a whore." Both versions contain a footnote indicating that the original Hebrew reads, "You son of a perverse and rebellious woman."

The NLT claims to be the "first adult-level Bible translated by evangelical scholars using the dynamic-equivalence (thought-for-thought) method of translation." Indeed, it is written on a sixth-grade reading level, which is considerably higher than the reading level of either the New Century Version or the Contemporary English Version. It contains sentences of greater length and complexity than either of these two other translations do. For this reason, it will find a receptive audience among adults who find themselves torn between the flow of verbal translations like the New International Version or the New King James Version and the simplicity of the New Century Version or Contemporary English Version.

The NET Bible

In November 1995 a group of biblical scholars met to discuss the possibility of developing a new translation specifically designed to be placed on the Internet. Part of their purpose was to provide a translation of the Bible done with scholarly integrity yet accessible to the public in every way possible. The result of almost four years' work was the NET Bible: New English Translation. Using standard Hebrew and Greek texts, these scholars took advantage of technological advances (e-mail, networks, and the Web) to create the translation in a relatively short period of time and to make it readily available to everyone with access to the Internet.

The NET Bible is a dynamic translation with an almost overwhelming number of notes. Some of these notes give information about text-critical issues; others involve interpretative issues; still others provide a literal translation when the editors and translators felt that the reader might benefit by comparing the published translation with a more verbal translation.

The NET Bible offers little that is new or radical in the way of translation. What is new or unique is its commitment to an electronic format as the primary format. A careful look at both the Web version and the print version of the NET Bible New Testament makes this commitment clear. In the print version the translation, textual, and grammatical notes are almost overwhelming to the reader. The Web version, with its links and frames, allows the reader to separate notes from the biblical text and to move rapidly between passages.

A number of strengths commend this version. First, it is a fairly comprehensive study Bible. The textual and translation notes are excellent and seem to carry little in the way of a hidden agenda. Second, the electronic format makes this version more available and affordable than most other recent translations of the Bible. The website allows for continuing discussion about the translation. Translators and editors can ask for and respond to comments and questions about the translation or notes by e-mail.

Some questions remain. First, the version claims to be useful for public reading as well as for serious Bible study, but the inclusion of so many notes is a distraction if one is simply trying to read the text. Second, some of the notes tend toward interpretative commentary, which may disturb readers who expected to find only a translation. While the introduction to the NET Bible admits to and explains this tendency, many readers will fail to take note of those introductory words. Finally, one has to wonder why the electronic text is not searchable. The ability to search for words in both the text of the translation and the notes would significantly enhance the usefulness of this version.

On the subject of gender-inclusive language, the NET Bible gets somewhat mixed reviews. On the one hand, this translation will not satisfy many of the participants in the inclusive-language conversation. For instance, even when trying to be inclusive the translators chose "mankind" rather than "humanity" (see John 1:4). On the other hand, the editors and translators are to be given credit for addressing this subject in their introduction. One may not agree with all the results, but at least the editors demonstrate their awareness and sensitivity.

On balance, this is a translation that every serious Bible student ought to take into consideration. That it is freely available might be enough to make the NET Bible a useful resource for many years to come. (For more information on the NET Bible, check the website at www.bible.org.)

Good News Bible: Today's English Version (TEV)

In the early 1960s, Eugene Nida, then Secretary of the Translations Department of the American Bible Society, became convinced of the need for a new type of translation. Impressed by the success of a Spanish version that was directed toward millions of indigenous peoples in Mexico, Central America, and South America, Nida proposed a new philosophy of dynamic translation. This common language approach to translation would be grounded in a thorough understanding of both the original languages and the modern languages involved. The American Bible Society, which had to that point printed only verbal translations, took up Nida's proposal. A sample translation of Mark's Gospel was prepared under the direction of Robert G. Bratcher, a research associate in the Translation Department. The enthusiastic response to this volume encouraged the Society to ask Bratcher to translate the entire New Testament.

Bratcher's translation was published in 1966 under the title Good News for Modern Man. This version quickly sold some twelve million copies. An Old Testament translation was then undertaken by a team of seven translators, most of whom had already assisted in the process of Bible translation in international mission contexts. The complete Bible was published in 1976 as the Good News Bible: Today's English Version.

The translation team adopted several guidelines. While they did not restrict the vocabulary to any certain grade level, the language of the TEV was intended to be "natural, clear, simple, and unambiguous." Names of persons and places were printed in their most familiar form. Yahweh (YHWH) was translated as simply "Lord."

Extensive reader's notes supplement the text, including cultural and historical notes, textual notes, alternative renderings, and references to other passages. Short introductions to each book are included, as well as a short outline. The appendixes consist of a word list, a chronological chart of major biblical events, an index, a list of Septuagint passages used in the New Testament, and maps.

Perhaps the most distinctive feature of the TEV is its line drawings, which drew mixed reviews. These were prepared by Annie Vallotton, a Swiss artist, and were intended to draw the reader into the text.

The 1976 edition of the TEV was an accurate and carefully constructed translation that usually succeeded in capturing the idiomatic flavor of the ancient Greek and Hebrew. Consider the following example from Psalm 23:1-3, "The Lᴏʀᴅ is my shepherd;/ I have everything I need./ He lets me rest in fields of green grass/ and leads me to quiet pools of fresh water./ He gives me new strength./ He guides me in the right paths/ as he has promised."

Careful pains were taken to modernize such words as *centurion, Publicans, Sanhedrin, raca, mammon,* and many others. Theological concepts like "justify" were translated into such simple phrases as "put right with God."

The 1976 edition of the TEV was roundly criticized in at least two areas. First, like most common-language translations, it oversimplifies certain complex passages. Second, like the Revised English Bible, it received mixed reviews in its attention to gender-inclusive language.

A revision of the TEV, published in 1992, gave more careful attention to inclusive language and to certain stylistic and exegetical problems that existed in the 1976 edition. It also removed the line drawings that had marked the earlier edition. The preface to the new edition states that "where references in particular passages are to both men and women, the revision aims at language that is not exclusively masculine-oriented. At the same time, however, great care was taken not to distort the historical situation of the ancient patriarchal culture of Bible times."

Psalm 8:4 provides a good example of the evolution of the TEV from 1976 to 1992:

1976 edition: "What is man, that you think of him; mere man, that you care for him?"
1992 edition: "What are human beings, that you think of them; mere mortals, that you care for them?"

The 1992 revision offered an essential corrective that makes the TEV a valuable tool for devotional study. Those persons who desire a simple, readable translation of the Bible will find it especially helpful.

Contemporary English Version (CEV)

Fortunately, the American Bible Society has not rested on its laurels. It has prepared a new translation, the Contemporary English Version, which is a worthy successor to its older sibling. The CEV began in the mind of Barclay Newman, who assisted in the translation of the Good News Bible. In the mid-1980s Newman began to study popular forms of the English language found in books, magazines, newspapers, and television to see what kind of language people were speaking and hearing. He was particularly concerned with how people heard texts when they were read aloud.

In 1986 he published a test volume that was a collection of illustrated Scripture passages for children. Its warm public reception encouraged Newman to translate the entire Bible. The New Testament was completed on the 175th anniversary of the American Bible Society in 1991. The entire Bible was published in 1995.

The public reading of the Bible was a primary concern of the CEV translators and led them to adopt three guiding principles for their translation. First, an experienced reader should be able to read it aloud easily without stumbling. Since most readers usually pause at the end of a line, attention was paid to line breaks in the text in order to reduce the possibility of misunderstanding on the part of the hearer. Second, it should be understood by someone with little familiarity with biblical language. And finally, it should be understood and enjoyed by English speakers regardless of their religious or educational background.

The CEV makes every effort at gender-inclusive language, except in the case of references to God. Genesis 1:26 ("humans") and 6:1 ("More and more people were born") provide examples of the careful and systematic use of such language throughout the translation.

Like Today's English Version, the CEV makes every effort to rid itself of complex theological language and "biblicisms." Such words as *righteo usness, redemption, atonement,* and *sanctification* are avoided in favor of simple phrases that express the same theological truth but in a much clearer fashion.

The removal of theological verbiage is perhaps the greatest contribution of the translation. The New International Version translates Romans 3:21 as "But now a righteousness from God, apart from the law, has been made known, to which the Law and the Prophets testify." The CEV reads: "Now we see how God does make us acceptable to him. The Law and the Prophets tell how we become acceptable, and it isn't by obeying the Law of Moses." For the most part the CEV accomplishes its goal of offering a readable common-language translation of the Bible free of theological jargon. Such an accomplishment is important in a time of rising illiteracy. The CEV places in the hands of the public a Bible translation that is beautiful in its simplicity and, more important, easily read and understood.

Paraphrases

Considerable debate has raged in recent years over the value of paraphrased versions of the Bible. This debate centers around the nature of the translation process. In many ways, all translations are paraphrases of the Bible, because no translation can ever capture the exact meaning of the original language. Certainly all dynamic translations of the Bible paraphrase in that translators provide expressions in the modern language that have similar meanings to expressions in the ancient language but that are not verbal equivalents.

The differences are more of degree than of type. Certain Bible versions are more concerned with communicating spiritual truth in everyday English than with remaining faithful to the exact meaning of the original language. These versions are best described as paraphrases. Unlike verbal and dynamic translations, paraphrases hope to express the underlying meaning rather than to render the individual words and phrases. A paraphrase is not to be considered inferior to a verbal or dynamic translation.

Two popular paraphrased versions of the Bible have been published in the late twentieth century. We have already introduced The Living Bible in our discussion of its descendant, the New Living

Modern Translations: Verbal, Dynamic, and Paraphrase

Translation. Without doubt The Living Bible dramatically transformed the popular view of the Bible upon its publication in 1971. A second paraphrase, entitled The Message, received an enthusiastic response when it was published by NavPress in 1993.

The Living Bible (LB)

When the LB appeared in the early 1970s, it sparked a revival of interest in the Bible, especially among young people. The LB's language seemed relevant to the younger generation, and the fact that it was a "paraphrase" gave it an alluring air. Many people credited the power of its language for their conversion to Christianity. By 1972 the LB was the best-selling non-fiction book in America, and by 1979 over twenty million copies had been sold.

But not everyone praised it. One conservative minister called the LB "the worst of all the different new Bibles that have been produced." And others were troubled by its straightforward sexual language, such as that found in Genesis 4:1: "Then Adam had sexual intercourse with Eve his wife, and she conceived and gave birth to a son."

At the center of this storm was Kenneth N. Taylor, a seminary-trained publisher, whose concern that the American Standard Version of 1901 was unintelligible to most Americans led him to undertake this revision of the English Bible. Taylor began work on the paraphrase in order to help his ten children understand the Bible. He hoped to restate the authors' thoughts "in different words than the author used" and to do so from a "rigid evangelical position."

Taylor's rigid evangelicalism (read "fundamentalism") is clearly evident in such passages as Galatians 5:11, Ephesians 3:21, and 1 Timothy 2:7 in which he uses the obviously evangelical phrase "plan of salvation" in the place of such phrases as "the offense of the cross" and "the true faith." Taylor sometimes diminishes the humanity of Jesus in favor of a strengthened divinity. For example, the phrase "I, the Messiah" is substituted for Jesus' description of himself as "Son of Man." Other kinds of textual manipulation also occur. Second

Samuel 21:19 identifies Elhanan son of Jaare-Oregim, and not David, as the man who killed Goliath the Gittite. Taylor fixes this problem up nicely by identifying Elhanan as the killer of the *brother* of Goliath the Gittite. One wonders how many other passages were altered to make all the Bible's stories correspond.

Does this mean that the LB should be avoided? Not at all. Taylor is to be praised for this successful effort, which more than any other recent event may be responsible for the Bible's wide popularity today. He is also to be commended for his early decision to set up a missionary foundation to receive the royalties from the LB. In addition, the success of the LB has enabled him to establish Tyndale House Publishers as a major force in the Christian publishing industry.

The Message

In 1993 Eugene H. Peterson's The Message, a paraphrase of the New Testament, hit bookstore shelves and quickly became a popular Bible version, especially among young people. Peterson, a Presbyterian pastor, had published a number of books in the field of Christian spirituality before turning his attention to the Bible. His work is reminiscent of J. B. Phillips's The New Testament in Modern English.

The Message has neither verse number designations nor the usual two-column standard biblical format. Its purpose is to recapture the vitality and power with which the Bible was first heard by ancient peoples. Peterson points out that the Bible was written in informal Greek, "the street language of the day, the idiom of the playground and marketplace." For this reason, he believes it should be rendered into English "not [as] a refined language that appeals to our aspirations after the best but a rough and earthy language that reveals God's presence and action where we least expect it."

The Message is free of any study aids or notes to assist in the interpretation of the text; the Bible appears readily accessible to its readers. A short introduction is provided at the beginning of each New Testament book.

Like The Living Bible, The Message must be approached with some caution. It is free of the obvious theological bias that characterizes the Living Bible, though translators cannot help importing their own perspectives into the text. Peterson's interest in spirituality is clear, because the text reads almost like a spiritual treatise that might have been written by an early church father or mother.

Its greatest fault is the result of the fact that it is a paraphrase. On many occasions Peterson adds short phrases to clear up confusion in the text. For example, in Matthew 1:18 he helps us to understand Joseph's confusion over Mary's pregnancy: "Before they came to the marriage bed, Joseph discovered she was pregnant. (It was by the Holy Spirit, but he didn't know that.)"

Peterson's use of idiomatic "street language" sometimes seems a bit forced. In Matthew 3:9, being a descendant of Abraham is described as being "neither here nor there." In Luke 19:7, when Jesus goes to the home of Zaccheus, people say of Jesus, "What business does he have getting cozy with this crook?" And in John 8:45 the Jewish leaders say, "That clinches it." Some renderings of particular verses are simply strange. For example, Peterson writes in Romans 15:13 "May the God of green hope fill you up with joy," and in Galatians 6:13, "All their talk about the law is gas."

The Message has filled a niche among Bible readers as a popular devotional Bible. And it is likely that this popularity will increase as people are attracted by its unorthodox appearance, unique style, and easy readability. But these very qualities make it unlikely that the paraphrase will ever become much more than an interesting curiosity in the world of Bible translations. The lack of verse number designations alone is enough to put off those who are looking for a Bible to use in group study or worship.

Conclusion

This evaluation and analysis of modern English translations brings us to the end of a journey that began in the ancient storytelling world of the Jewish people. We have discovered that the concerns of those ancient storytellers are much like the concerns of Bible translators today. Contemporary translators must retell the ancient stories of the Bible in such a way that those stories meet the spiritual needs of our day. The task is not easy.

But translation remains only part of the process. In an effort to appeal to every possible reader, Bible publishers have added what we will call formats to the text of the Bible. Choosing a Bible now means deciding on a format as well as on a translation. Our next chapter offers a practical guide to many of the formats available today.

3

"Formatting" the Bible

Choosing a translation is only the first step in purchasing a Bible. Today's Bibles, like almost everything else, come in many different colors, shapes, and sizes. We call this phenomenon "formatting" the Bible. Choosing a Bible involves both deciding on a translation or version and deciding on how you want that translation to be packaged.

The Bible remains a consistent best-seller. Therefore, many publishing companies have adopted two strategies with regard to Bible publication and sales. First, new translations and versions have been developed. Second, every possible market for the Bible has been explored. The result of this second strategy is the publication of Bibles in different formats, each format designed to appeal to a specific segment of the market.

Choosing a Bible demands that you be informed about both the translation and the format that you are about to purchase and use. This chapter provides information to make you a better consumer. We have divided the formats into three categories similar to those used by Christian publishers and booksellers: study Bibles, specialty Bibles, and children's and youth Bibles. Our goal is to examine some of the popular sellers in each category and provide you with an honest and clear evaluation of each format.

Study Bibles

Bibles in this category have notes and other features that are designed to help the reader come to a clearer understanding of the text or lead to deeper thought and study. This is a rather broad category, including both scholarly and devotional Bibles.

The Amplified Bible

Published between 1958 and 1965, The Amplified Bible was a joint project of the Lockman Foundation and Zondervan Publishing House. The original concept was developed by Frances E. Siewert, who hoped to produce a version that would offer the modern reader a sense of the range of meanings embedded in the words of the ancient languages. Although it is a verbal translation, the Amplified Bible contributes to understanding of Scripture by its survey of a range of meanings for each word. As we have noted, translation often involves choosing just one word or phrase among many to express the ancient word in modern English. The Amplified Bible intentionally abandons the limits of word-for-word translation, listing in the text other translation options.

If you are going to own just one Bible, this is probably not the one to choose. If you decide to buy a second Bible, though, the Amplified Bible should receive careful consideration. It does an excellent job of expressing the range of meanings that an ancient reader might have "heard" in the words of Scripture.

Cambridge Annotated Study Bible
(New Revised Standard Version)

Any Bible with the word *annotated* in its title is probably at the scholarly end of the spectrum. This format, based on the New Revised Standard Version, incorporates the work of Howard Clark Kee, an internationally acclaimed biblical scholar who has enjoyed a long and fruitful career of teaching, publishing, and speaking. Following a standard annotated format, the volume begins with an introduction to the Bible, including a summary of the development of the biblical canon, and introductions to individual books found in the Protestant canon. The text follows this introduction, accompanied by Kee's notes in the outside margins, biblical cross-references in the inside margins, and textual footnotes. The biblical text is followed by a glossary and Bible maps in color, as well as by other tools for serious Bible study.

Published in 1993, this volume benefits from the richness of Kee's career. The notes are relatively free of personal bias; they are clear and add much to the reader's understanding of the text. The introductory material is also clear, concise, and very helpful. Perhaps the only drawback to this volume is that it depends on one scholar, whereas other annotated volumes contain the work of teams of scholars.

The Catholic Study Bible (New American Bible)

Published in 1990 by Oxford University Press, this volume contains some of the best Roman Catholic biblical scholarship presented in a format that makes it available to a wide audience. The study Bible begins with general and introductory articles. Reading guides make up the majority of the introductory material: There is an introduction to each section of both testaments, and the reader is given helpful suggestions for reading Scripture. The text of the New American Bible follows; each book is preceded by a short introduction and is accompanied by translation and interpretative footnotes. The biblical text is followed by reference articles, including a glossary, articles on the lectionary, articles on biblical archaeology and history, and color maps.

This volume combines a fine translation with some excellent biblical scholarship. It offers valuable tools for Roman Catholics, but it will benefit all readers. A personal edition (1995) is particularly helpful for individual study.

The HarperCollins Study Bible
(New Revised Standard Version)

Published in 1993, this volume represents the combined efforts of over sixty biblical scholars under the sponsorship of the Society of Biblical Literature (an international organization of biblical scholars).

Following a short introduction by General Editor Wayne A. Meeks, this study Bible presents the New Revised Standard Version translation, including the apocryphal books. Each book is preceded by a short introduction and accompanied by extensive notes on the biblical text. Numerous black-and-white maps and tables are incorporated into the text of the biblical books; color maps and a table of Old Testament quotations found in New Testament texts follow the biblical text. This is a very good choice for anyone seeking a study Bible. The notes are clear and numerous; they are also the product of a team of scholars. A weakness in this study Bible lies in the decision not to include more in the way of material that introduces the Bible and its history.

The Inspirational Study Bible (New Century Version)

Published in 1995 by Word Publishing, this volume is edited by Max Lucado and is subtitled "Life Lessons from the Inspired Word of God." Using the text of the New Century Version, Lucado and a team of editors offer "helpful tools to expand your understanding" of Scripture. Each book is prefaced with an introduction by Lucado. A series of "Life Lessons" follow in the outside margins of the biblical text: The "Situation" analyzes the context of the chapter; the "Observation" explains the truth or lesson in the chapter; then the "Inspiration" offers an excerpt from a Christian writer; the "Application" suggests how to apply the lessons to the reader's life; and the "Exploration" refers to other Scripture passages with the same theme. Following the biblical text are several devotional and study aids, including a topical index to devotional thought and readings, reading plans, and a dictionary/topical concordance.

This is not an annotated, scholarly study Bible. Lucado and his team intend this volume to be an aid in deepening one's devotional life, and this format is successful in meeting that aim. People who enjoy Lucado's writings will enjoy this volume.

Life Application Study Bible (several versions)

A joint project of Tyndale House Publishers and Zondervan Publishing House, this format is based on notes and Bible helps developed for Youth for Christ/USA. It is intended to help readers apply the Bible to their daily living. The volume contains application notes at the bottom of the page throughout the biblical text. These notes have three parts: an "Explanation" connecting the application to the Scripture passage; a "Bridge" making the "timeless truth . . . relevant for today"; and an "Application" showing how to apply the "timeless truth" to the reader's life. Other features include explanatory notes, an introduction to each book (containing a timeline, vital statistics, an overview, an outline, "megathemes," and a map), profiles of biblical characters, maps (many scattered throughout the text), charts and diagrams, an index, and a dictionary.

This is one of the most popular formats available. Many features of this volume are helpful, particularly the material introducing each biblical book and placing it in canonical and historical context. It has a conservative slant, as evidenced in the notes and other material (for example, the character highlighted in Ruth is Boaz, not Ruth). The primary purpose of the features is to aid Christian devotion and practice.

The MacArthur Study Bible (New King James Version)

This volume, published by Word Publishing in 1997, contains the notes of John MacArthur, president of the Master's Seminary and host of the "Grace to You" radio program. A relatively short introductory section precedes the biblical text in the New King James Version and MacArthur's notes. A fairly comprehensive topical index, some notes on the character of true saving faith, a theological overview, a table of weights and monies, and color maps follow the texts. Other charts and maps are included throughout the volume, and each biblical book is preceded by a short introduction.

Choose this study Bible if you agree with and like MacArthur's writings, which are conservative and premillennial. The notes are informative, especially as devotional aids.

The Nelson Study Bible (New King James Version)

Introduced in 1997 by Thomas Nelson Publishers, this volume claims to be the "finest Study Bible ever." It includes introductions to each book, translators' notes, and scholarly notes to the New King James Version of the biblical text. These features are incorporated into the text, making it very useable for the reader. The biblical text is preceded by a short introduction on how to study the Bible and an extended table of contents that provides page numbers of various in-text features. These features include "FullView Bible Summaries" (full-page, color, thematic articles), "InDepth Articles" (expanding on a thought or event), "Quick-View Charts," "InText Maps" (black-and-white), and "WordFocus Word Studies" (keyed to the *Strong's Concordance* numbering system). The volume concludes with a subject index, a concordance, and color maps.

This volume combines solid conservative scholarship with a pastoral or devotional aim. The inclusion of charts, maps, articles, and word studies in the biblical text is a good idea. The work seems cluttered, though, almost as if the other features overshadow the Bible text.

The NIV Study Bible (New International Version)

Published in 1985 and 1995 (10th anniversary edition) by Zondervan Publishing House, this volume builds on the popularity of the New International Version. As introductory material this volume includes a full-color chronological table, an introduction, and an overview of ancient texts relating to the Old Testament. With the text are study notes, the New International Version's cross-reference system, introductions to each biblical book, maps, charts, and a series of essays on biblical and ethical topics. The 1995 version also includes icons (or pictures) to highlight notes on characters, archaeological information, or personal application. Following the biblical text are a table of weights and measures; indexes to the subjects, notes, and maps; a concordance; and several color maps.

The strength of this study Bible lies in its use of the New International Version as well as in notes written by recognized evangelical scholars. The notes incorporate conservative scholarship without being slanted toward any one person's point of view. If you are looking for solid conservative scholarship without too many frills and you are sold on the New International Version, choose this format.

The New Oxford Annotated Bible
(New Revised Standard Version)

The Oxford Annotated Bible (published in the 1960s using the Revised Standard Version) remains one of the standard critical tools of biblical scholarship. With the advent of the New Revised Standard Version came the New Oxford Annotated Bible (1991). All of the articles in the original format were reviewed and edited; new articles were added where necessary, and some articles were replaced to incorporate scholarly advances. The articles and notes come from a team of reputable scholars representing ecumenical Christianity. The volume includes introductory notes to the Old Testament, the Apocrypha, and the New Testament, as well as study notes answering interpretative and textual questions. General articles include "Modern Approaches to Biblical Study," "Characteristics of Hebrew Poetry," "Literary Forms in the Gospels," "English Versions of the Bible," "Survey of the Geography, History, and Archaeology of the Bible Lands," and "Measures and Weights."

In terms of presenting the fruits of biblical scholarship, only the HarperCollins Study Bible and the original Oxford Annotated Bible compare to this format. This volume continues to represent the best of British and North American biblical scholarship. That is not to say that it is free of bias; its notes will not always agree with those of conservative or evangelical study Bibles. The general articles are excellent, as are the color maps. Like other annotated study Bibles, the emphasis in this volume is on the text and notes rather than on other tools or on devotional application.

Praise and Worship Study Bible (New Living Translation)

Published in 1997 by Tyndale House Publishers, this volume filters Bible study through the lenses of praise and worship. It is

67

intended to aid readers in their understanding and practice of worship, using the New Living Translation of the Bible as a manual. Special features include introductions to biblical books that focus on worship themes, worship notes (meditations on a name or characteristic of God found in Scripture), worship profiles (learning about worship from biblical characters), hymns of faith (traditional and contemporary), symbols of worship (explanations and illustrations), prayers of the church, and charts. The volume begins with an essay tracing the theme of worship throughout the Scriptures, and the biblical text follows, with the features noted above interspersed throughout. It ends with an essay on the Christian year and indexes to the various features (hymns, symbols, prayers, etc.).

This format is rather limited. If your study Bible will be your main (or only) Bible, this is not the one to choose. If, however, you already own one or more Bibles and you are looking for a devotional aid, this volume offers some interesting features that may be quite helpful in learning about and practicing the worship of God.

The Quest Study Bible (New International Version)

This volume, introduced in 1994 by Zondervan Publishing House, is the result of collaboration between Zondervan and the editors of *Christianity Today* and *Leadership* magazines. Based on the New International Version, the format includes questions raised by readers of the biblical text (these questions were tested through nationwide focus-group research), book introductions, timelines and charts, explanatory articles, a dictionary, a concordance, color maps, and various indexes. The primary feature of this volume, though, is the series of side-column questions that address perplexing words and phrases, cultural contexts, reasons for God's actions, summaries of controversial passages, explanations of "peculiar" types of writing, and related passages.

These questions should be of interest to most readers. The answers are clear, well-written, and accessible to a lay audience. For the most part they represent accepted conservative positions. The only real weakness of this format is that the questions appear to obscure the biblical text.

Ryrie Study Bible: Expanded Edition (several versions)

Published in the mid 1990s by Moody Press, these editions of Charles C. Ryrie's Study Bible have been updated with some new notes and other added features. They are based on the work of Ryrie, a long-time professor at Dallas Theological Seminary, and showcase his introduction to each book and study notes keyed to chapters and verses. The biblical text also includes outline headings, and the book introductions include outlines, timelines, and other charts. Some charts and black-and-white maps have been included in the text. Essays and indexes follow the biblical text, including a subject index, a synopsis of biblical doctrine, an essay on the inspiration of the Bible, and even a survey of Christian history.

Ryrie is one of the leading proponents of the dispensational premillennial interpretation of Christian history and the Bible, a stance that often colors his notes and heavily flavors the appended essays and timelines. Most of the time Ryrie agrees with other conservative interpreters, but his notes will rarely suggest that other interpretations also exist.

NAB New Testament: Saint Joseph Edition
(New American Bible)

Published by Catholic Book Publishers, this study Bible is designed for North American Roman Catholic readers. Its features include an introductory essay on how to read the Bible and other essays on the history of the New Testament and its canon. An annotated New Testament forms the bulk of this volume, with the notes and introductions to each book provided by Kathryn Sullivan of the Sisters of the Sacred Heart. Charts, a study guide to the New Testament, a guide to the Sunday Gospel readings, and a dictionary make up the remainder of the book.

This format has much to recommend it. The notes are generally of high quality, and they do not interfere with reading the text. The book introductions are brief, but they are clear and informative.

The New Scofield Reference Bible (King James Version)

Convinced that the Bible holds the key to prophecies about the return of Jesus and the endtimes, C. I. Scofield published his notes to the King James Version in 1909; they were revised in 1917. In these notes he laid out an elaborate chronology of dispensations, or ages, that define salvation history. Revised again in the 1960s, the Scofield Bible remains the classic statement of dispensational premillennialism. This volume contains introductions to each biblical book (including chronology) and Scofield's notes. Following the biblical text is an index, a concordance, and color maps.

Choose this format if you are interested in Scofield's perspective on biblical prophecy or in conservative biblical scholarship of the early 1900s. Be aware that this is a classic, and many of the other study Bibles will already have taken Scofield's arguments into account as they annotate the text.

Serendipity Bible (New International Version)

Introduced in 1986 by Serendipity House and Zondervan Publishing House, this format, based on the New International Version, has been updated in a tenth anniversary edition. Aimed at small groups, the original edition offered discussion questions connected with the biblical text and designed to lead groups into serious discussion. These study and discussion questions and the book introductions have been updated in the new edition.

The volume contains an introduction to the small group Bible study process and sixty ready-made courses of study from which groups can choose (men, women, singles, marriage, parenting, youth, marketplace, spiritual, special needs, and recovery courses). The biblical text is followed by a list of 200 favorite Bible stories, group study courses, a chart of readings for the church year, a subject index, and a dictionary/concordance.

If you are looking for a Bible to use for group Bible study, this is an excellent option, especially if everyone in the group has a copy.

The Thompson Chain-Reference Bible (several versions)

First published at about the same time as Scofield's Bible, this format was the result of considerable study on the part of Frank Charles Thompson and Laura Boughton Thompson. The volume contains introductions to each book, outline studies, biographical studies, Bible harmonies, an archaeological supplement, a concordance, and color maps. The heart of this format, though, is the series of marginal references that—chained together—aid the reader in tracing themes and ideas throughout both testaments.

Choose this format if you are interested in tracing themes through the Bible. A good concordance may serve you just as well.

Specialty Bibles

In recent years a spate of specialty Bibles has appeared on bookstore shelves. These Bibles target groups of people within the general population or address particular needs that people might have as they study the Bible. Whether addressing the specific needs of women, men, couples, people in recovery, teenagers, students, or persons of the same cultural heritage, these Bibles are designed to connect the biblical message with the spiritual needs of particular segments of the culture.

The Original African Heritage Study Bible
(King James Version)

The Original African Heritage Study Bible, published in 1993 by James C. Winston Publishing Company, sets out "to interpret the Bible as it relates specifically to persons of African descent and thereby to foster an appreciation of the multiculturalism inherent in the Bible." This format, based on the King James Version, highlights the central role of African peoples in God's salvation history.

James W. Peebles, president of Winston-Derek Publishing Group, spearheaded this effort. He contends that most Bible translations have failed to give credit to African peoples for their contributions to Judaism and to Christianity. And so he gathered an ecumenical group of scholars from a wide range of Christian denominations to author supplementary articles to the King James text on topics ranging from multiculturalism in Scripture to martyrdom of African Christians to African women and Scripture. The format even includes some twenty-four songs born out of the African slave experience in the United States and photographs and paintings of Africans dressed as biblical characters. Cain Hope Felder, professor of New Testament Language and Literature at Howard University, served as general editor for the project.

Textual notes and appended articles draw attention to Africa as the site of the earliest human civilization, pointing out that the boundaries of the garden of Eden stretched into modern-day Ethiopia. Adam and Eve are identified as "African/Edenic peoples." Notes attached to Matthew's genealogy connect Jesus to the "Hamitic line" through Rahab.

Peebles and his team of ecumenical scholars are to be commended for this specialty Bible. It offers a corrective to the Euro-American biases of many modern translations and formats. At the same time, however, it substitutes one kind of bias for another, often exaggerating the kinship ties between the ancient Africans and the ancient Israelites. Perhaps its greatest contribution is the reminder that the biblical story is intended for all human cultures.

Couples' Devotional Bible (New International Version)

The Couples' Devotional Bible, published by the Zondervan Publishing House in 1994, weaves daily devotional readings for married couples together with the New International Version. These devotional readings are interspersed throughout the text and contain questions "designed to help you and your spouse talk about real issues within your own unique marriage relationship."

The Couples' Devotional Bible was edited by the staff of *Marriage Partnership* magazine, an evangelical Christian publication, who invited some 120 popular Christian speakers, writers, and seminar leaders to write the daily devotions. Each devotional contains a verse and passage for the day, a reading, a question section entitled "Marriage Builders," and some additional Scripture passages. The readings are organized by days of the week; a number at the bottom of each page indicates the location of the next reading. The *Marriage Partnership* staff authored special "Weekending" sections for Saturday and Sunday. A reading plan, author biographies, and a subject index are included in appendixes.

This format offers a well-balanced series of devotionals by Christian writers from nearly every corner of the evangelical Christian world. Contributors include Frederick Buechner, Will Willimon, Charles Colson, Bill and Gloria Gaither, Ruth Bell Graham, and Max Lucado. Couples who are seeking a Bible that offers a focal point for deepening their relationship will be pleased by this one.

Family Walk Devotional Bible (New International Version)

The Family Walk Devotional Bible, based on the New International Version, includes topical studies taken from *Family Walk,* a monthly magazine published by Walk Thru the Bible Ministries (WTB). The mission of WTB is to communicate the central themes of Scripture and their practical application. Founded by Bruce Wilkinson, WTB Ministries designed the Family Walk Bible to help families discover how God relates to their world.

Like the Couples' Devotional Bible, this family-oriented format, also published by The Zondervan Corporation (1996), contains daily devotional readings that address family concerns and issues. Topics include creation, wisdom, security, and mercy; the focus is on matters that concern 5-12 year-old children. Some devotionals raise questions; other devotionals encourage the writing down of responses to particular passages. Full-color pages entitled "Big Questions" have been interspersed throughout the text to answer such concerns as "What is the Bible?" and "Where is Jesus now?" Each biblical book is preceded by a short introduction to its basic message and context. A reading plan and subject index are included in the appendix.

This Bible is an obvious choice for conservative and evangelical Christian families who are interested in a family devotional time or family altar.

The Life Recovery Bible (New Living Translation)

This volume directs readers to the "resources for recovery found in the Holy Scriptures." Published using The Living Bible in 1992 by Tyndale House and reprinted using the New Living Translation in late 1998, The Life Recovery Bible includes a number of helpful features for persons in Alcoholics Anonymous or other recovery groups patterned after AA. This Bible is user-friendly, with three devotional reading plans (Twelve-Step Plan, Recovery Principle Plan, and Serenity Prayer Plan) interspersed throughout the biblical text. Each plan contains a number of devotional readings that are tied to specific biblical passages related to recovery.

Other helpful features are included in this format. Recovery profiles of biblical characters draw attention to the ways in which about eighty individuals overcame significant life challenges. Introductory materials for specific Bible books, recovery commentary notes, and an index assist readers as well.

Stephen Arterburn and David Stoop, two clinicians who have written extensively in the area of recovery, serve as editors. Offering a source of encouragement to people in recovery, the volume provides a constant reminder of God's presence, the consequences of actions, the common plight of humanity, and the reality of forgiveness.

Men's Devotional Bible (New International Version)

This volume is another in Zondervan's New International Version devotional series. Published in 1993, the Men's Devotional Bible is designed to help men "discover the Biblical model of masculinity and maturity." Its features include daily devotional readings interspersed throughout the text, introductions to each Bible book, a plan for reading the Bible through in its entirety, biographies of devotional writers, and a subject index directed toward the specific needs of men. The latest edition was published in 1997.

Like Zondervan's other devotional Bibles, this one draws its devotional authors from a cross-section of the evangelical world. Writers include Pat Boone, Charles Colson, Larry Burkett, Tony Campolo, Frederick Buechner, and Billy Graham.

My Utmost Devotional Bible (King James Version)

My Utmost Devotional Bible weaves together the devotional writings of Oswald Chambers and the King James Version. First published by Thomas Nelson Publishers in 1992, this volume offers daily readings that include a meditation by Chambers, texts from the Old and New Testaments (designed to take the reader through the Bible in one year), and special quotations related to the biblical passages. The latest edition was printed in 1997.

Chambers was a Scottish Christian evangelist whose devotional books were assembled by his wife after his untimely death in Egypt during World War I. His best-known work is the classic *My Utmost for His Highest.*

Features of this devotional Bible include a short introduction and indexes to the various meditations. It is a wonderful resource for persons who wish to read the Bible through in a single year using the King James Version.

Nave's Topical Bible (King James Version)

Nave's Topical Bible, edited by Orville J. Nave and first printed in 1896, is best described as an encyclopedia of biblical passages. It arranges biblical passages by subject heading and also identifies biblical names and geographic locations. An appended index provides the page number for every Bible verse. Nave prepared this topical Bible while serving as a chaplain in the U.S. Army. He described his work as "the result of fourteen years of delightful and untiring study of the Word of God."

Nave's Topical Bible has gone through numerous revisions and reprints, and today it is available on many Bible-related websites. The latest book edition was published in 1999 by Zondervan Publishing House.

The New Believer's Bible (New Living Translation)

The New Believer's Bible: First Steps for New Christians describes the Bible as the " 'user's manual of life' that we all have been searching for." It is designed for new Christians in the evangelical tradition who wish to deepen their spiritual lives and gain a basic understanding of the essential beliefs of Christianity. It is based on the New Living Translation and was published in 1996 by Tyndale House.

Helpful features include four reading tracks interspersed throughout the biblical text. These tracks focus on "Cornerstones" (the foundations of faith), "First Steps," "Off and Running," (everyday living) and "Big Questions" (difficult concerns). Additional helps include a guide to Bible study, a list of fifty-two great Bible stories with their main lessons, an overview of the Bible, a list of memory verses, a section on prophecies about Jesus, and a glossary of Christian terms like *atonement* and *justification.*

The New Believer's Bible offers a helpful introduction to the basic beliefs of Christianity from an evangelical Christian perspective.

The One-Year Bible (several versions)

The One-Year Bible contains 365 daily Bible readings from the Old Testament, New Testament, Psalms, and Proverbs. These four sections of the Bible are read in order, beginning with the first chapters of each section. The One-Year Bible originally included texts from The Living Bible. It is now available in the New Living Translation, the King James Version, the New American Standard Bible, the New International Version, and the New King James Version.

The Passages of Life Bible (New King James Version)

The Passages of Life Bible, published by Thomas Nelson in 1995, "integrates faith with real life issues, and speaks to men and women who want to move onward and upward in their spiritual lives." According to the dust jacket, it is intended for those neither young nor old who have come to understand the complexities and challenges of life. In other words, it is a Bible for middle age.

Edited by Dale Hanson Bourke, this volume includes some 200 short articles by various Christian writers that address the spiritual and practical concerns of middle-aged people. Sample articles include "Creative Grandparenting," "Coping with Divorce," and "Mentoring is a Two-way Street." The articles are placed in close proximity to the biblical passage on which they are based. A number of portraits of biblical characters are included. An appendix contains a concordance, a Bible reading plan, and personal journal pages.

The cover of this Bible states that it contains "timeless truth for every stage of spiritual maturity." In fact, it targets the spiritual needs of baby boomers. And it is that generation that will find it to be a helpful spiritual resource.

Promise Keepers Men's Study Bible (two versions)

The Promise Keepers Men's Study Bible, published by Zondervan in 1997, is designed for men who belong to the popular Christian men's movement called Promise Keepers. In the general introduction we read that the purpose of the Bible is to help men "gain confidence and competence in . . . seven areas of life," a reference to the seven promises of intimacy with God, brotherhood, faithfulness, servanthood, honor, unity, and mission that members pledge to keep. These promises are listed in the opening pages of the volume.

Other features include the Promise Keeper's Statement of Faith, an article entitled "Man-to-Man: About Being a Son of God," a two-track reading plan connected to the seven promises (one with commentary notes and one without), introductions to each biblical book, brief in-text notes, and in-depth articles on certain passages. A

"PromiseFinder Index," weights and measures table, dictionary, subject index, and concordance are appended. This format is available in both the King James Version and the New International Version.

The Promise Keepers Men's Study Bible will be quite helpful for men who are active in the Promise Keepers movement. Others may find its close affiliation with the movement to be more of a hindrance than a help.

Serenity: A Companion for Twelve-Step Recovery (New King James Version)

Serenity: A Companion for Twelve Step Recovery, based on the New King James Version of the New Testament, Psalms, and Proverbs, is another Bible designed for persons in recovery. Edited by Robert Hemfeldt, a psychologist, and Richard Fowler, a counselor, *Serenity* assists persons "in restoring . . . addictive and compulsive areas of your life to proper balance and perspective." It contains an introduction to recovery principles, the Serenity Prayer, a commentary on each of the twelve steps, and devotionals that are connected to each step. Biblical passages are shaded and identified by the step number with which they are concerned.

Serenity's small size, numerous features, and attractive format make it a Bible that persons in recovery will find useful. Its main limitation is that it does not include the Old Testament, except for Psalms and Proverbs.

The Spirit-Filled Life Bible (New King James Version)

The Spirit-Filled Life Bible represents the first effort to produce a transdenominational study Bible for persons from Pentecostal/charismatic traditions. Published by Thomas Nelson Publishers in 1991, this Bible is designed to "contribute to the ongoing stream of the Holy Spirit's workings today and tomorrow." To that end, scholars from some twenty Pentecostal/charismatic traditions and independent fellowships prepared articles and notes that highlight the role of the Holy Spirit in the Christian life. The latest edition appeared in 1997.

This volume contains three kinds of in-text notes: "Kingdom Dynamics," "Word Wealth," and "Truth-in-Action." All three types of notes are shaded to attract the reader's attention. "Kingdom Dynamics" outlines the basic principles of Christian faith, including everything from prayer to spiritual warfare. "Word Wealth" clarifies the meanings of particular words within the text. And "Truth-In-Action" connects in chart form the truths of various passages with the actions that should emerge from those truths.

Articles address such topics as "Bridging the Testaments," "Dealing with 'Last Things,'" and "The Holy Spirit and Restoration." Pat Robertson contributed an essay entitled "Spiritual Answers to Hard Questions." A concordance and map sections are also included. Notes on the biblical text clarify the meaning of words and phrases and seem particularly concerned to locate parallels between the biblical text and Pentecostal/charismatic worship practices and beliefs. For this reason persons from those traditions will find the volume helpful.

Women's Devotional Bible 2 (several versions)

Another of Zondervan's devotional Bibles, the Women's Devotional Bible 2 assists women to "discover how relevant God's Word is to your life today." This second volume of the popular series, published in 1995, contains a new set of devotionals by well-known Christian women and married couples. It also includes book introductions, a reading plan, author biographies, and a subject index. It is available in the New International Version, the King James Version, and the New Revised Standard Version.

Devotional writings are taken from historical personalities like Susannah Wesley; women known for their courage like Mother Teresa, Rosa Parks, and Corrie Ten Boom; and writers like Ruth Bell Graham and Catherine Marshall.

Children's and Youth Bibles

Another trend in Bible publishing is evident in the number of children's and youth or student Bibles that have recently appeared in bookstores. These Bibles come in formats designed with the younger reader in mind.

The Adventures in Odyssey Bible
(International Children's Bible)

Touting itself as the "most kid-friendly Bible ever," The Adventures in Odyssey Bible sets out "to introduce children to the importance of applying the Bible to their lives." The volume is a joint production of Focus on the Family and Word Publishing, and uses familiar characters from the "Adventures in Odyssey" radio program and the *Adventures in Odyssey* cartoon video series.

Published by Word in 1994 and again in 1996, this Bible uses the International Children's Bible, the first Bible translation ever created especially for children. It also includes special sections within the text that are set off by such characters as Mr. Whittaker of Whit's End, Dylan and Jessie Taylor, their friends Sal and Carter, and Mr. Whitaker's assistant, Eugene.

Small boxes called "Whit's Wisdom" draw attention to important lessons from the Bible. The "Imagination Station" leads young readers along a path of discovery about special biblical ideas. "Strataflyer Notes" are designed to take children on a journey to identify biblical characters, events, creatures, or places. Mini-comic inserts, memory verses, and character drop-ins are also scattered throughout. These many features make this Bible an attractive addition to the bookshelves of children between the ages of 8 and 11.

The New Adventure Bible (several versions)

"Welcome to the great adventure of reading, exploring and discovering the Bible for yourself." With these words, The New Adventure Bible invites older children to user-friendly Bible study using the New International Version, the King James Version, or the New Revised Standard Version. Published by Zondervan in 1989 and again in 1994, this Bible contains a number of interesting features that make it a practical and useful children's Bible. A leather edition was published in 1997.

Key verses for memorization are identified in colorful type. Full-page inserts provide information on major biblical characters, the origins of the Bible, prayer, and other relevant issues. "Life in Bible Times" sections are scattered throughout the text and address the cultural realities of the ancient world. "Did You Know" boxes assist children to higher levels of biblical literacy. "Let's Live It" sections help children to use questions and activities to discover how the Bible can influence their work, play, and life. Other features include book introductions, an index, a list of activities, a dictionary/ concordance, charts, and maps.

While The New Adventure Bible is a good children's Bible, its use of the New International Version, the King James Version, and the New Revised Standard Version makes it less child-friendly than The Adventures in Odyssey Bible. For this reason, The New Adventure Bible should be used by children who are at least 10 years old.

Holy Bible: NIrV Kids' Study Bible
(New International Reader's Version)

The NIrV Kids' Study Bible uses the text of the New International Reader's Version, a translation designed for children, adults just learning to read, and people who are reading the Bible for the very first time. Published by Zondervan, this Bible contains colorful full-page pictures of biblical events; sections entitled "Think About This," which raise questions about nearby readings; study helps called "Look at This," which invite attention to interesting pictures; and sections entitled "Remember This," designed to give practical help in daily living.

Other features include introductions to the books of the Bible, an essay entitled "Life in New Testament Times," and a dictionary. The NIrV translation is designed to be accessible to those who read at a fourth-grade level or below. For this reason, The NIrV Kids' Study Bible will be helpful to children between 7 and 9 years of age, who will be attracted by its cover and by the wonderful pictures of biblical events and people.

Student's Life Application Bible (New Living Translation)

The purpose of the Student's Life Application Bible, published by Tyndale House in 1992 and again in 1994, is "to help you understand and apply God's Word." Designed for teens, it contains a number of in-text helps along with a Bible reading plan, a course on the basics of Christian faith, indexes to life topics, in-text notes, and well-known Bible stories.

This Bible's pages are filled with special in-text features, including book introductions, personality profiles, statistics, charts, maps, highlighted memory verses, moral dilemma and ultimate issue notes, "Here's What I did" notes, theme summaries of Bible books, and life application notes. These features hold the attention of high school and college students.

The Student's Life Application Bible is perfect for teenagers and young adults who are looking for an accessible and easily readable Bible format. However, this Bible contains so many in-text features that often it is difficult to separate the biblical text from the notes that surround it.

The Student Bible (several versions)

The Student Bible, first published by Zondervan in 1986, is a highly popular Bible among high school and college students and young adults. This Bible was developed by best-selling authors Philip Yancey and Tim Stafford and was revised in 1996.

Features in the revised edition include a three-track reading plan that enables readers to proceed through the Bible at their own pace, introductions to Bible books, in-text study articles called "Insights" and "Highlights," and a feature entitled "100 People You Should Know," which identifies major biblical characters. An expanded subject guide, a listing of biblical events, a glossary of non-biblical people and events mentioned in study helps, and color maps round out the format.

The Student Bible is designed to encourage the reading of Scripture on the part of younger adults and students. If popularity and sales are any indication, then this Bible is achieving its goal.

The Teen Study Bible (New International Version)

The Teen Study Bible is another of Zondervan's study Bibles that targets a younger audience. First published in 1993, this volume was revised and updated in 1999. Larry and Sue Richards wrote the in-text notes and other features.

The Teen Study Bible describes its purpose as putting teenagers "not just through God's Word but *into* it." Its many features include book introductions designed to connect the book to the life of a teenager and sections entitled "Direct Line," "Dear Sam," "Quizzer," and "Bible Promises." "Direct Line" is concerned with the struggles teenagers face. "Dear Sam" is an advice column sprinkled through the text. "Quizzer" offers Bible trivia questions. And "Bible Promises" offers insight into the promises of the Scriptures for teenagers. Jericho Joe is a cartoon character who adds a bit of humor to Bible study. A reading plan and subject index are appended.

The Teen Study Bible is an attractive Bible format that will appeal to many teenagers. The clear separation of notes from the biblical text gives it a slight advantage over the Student's Life Application Bible.

Youth Walk Devotional Bible (New International Version)

Published by Walk Thru the Bible Ministries (WTB) in 1992 and again in 1997, the Youth Walk Devotional Bible uses the New International Version translation to target a teenaged audience. Its features are similar to those contained in the Family Walk Devotional Bible, also published by WTB. Its stated purpose is "to help you discover how God relates to the world you live in today."

Features include daily devotions scattered through the text, introductions to Bible books, "Hot Topic" sections at the front and back of the volume, and "What Would Jesus Do? (WWJD)" sections that focus attention on ethical issues. An index and a reading plan are appended.

The Youth Walk Devotional Bible is exactly what it claims to be— a devotional Bible. Teenagers who are looking for study aids should choose one of the study Bibles listed above.

Conclusion

We hope this review of some Bible formats will help you in the process of choosing a Bible that will meet your specific spiritual needs. Again, don't be deterred by the vast number of Bibles on a bookstore shelf. Gather the essential information and ask some important questions. What questions? We will offer some suggestions in the next chapter.

4

Choosing and Using a Translation

We hope that the Bibles on the bookstore shelf have become a bit more familiar to you. But your problem remains the same: What Bible should you choose? To this point our purpose has been primarily to give you important information, but we haven't given you much help in making a decision about a Bible. This chapter is about making that decision. What Bible should you choose? How do you go about deciding? And what do you do with that Bible once you have it?

Choosing a Translation

We hope you were not expecting us to tell you which Bible is the "best" or the "right" translation, because no single translation can make such a claim. Because so many excellent translations and versions of the Bible are available, such a choice must take into account individual preferences as well as the relative strengths and weaknesses of each version. With that in mind, we offer the following questions that can assist you as you make your choice.

Who Will Be Using the Bible?

Bible translation and publishing is big business, and translations have become more specialized in order to attract a certain portion of the market. A Bible must fit the person, just as clothes must fit. This can be frustrating, especially if you are choosing a Bible for someone else. One way to reduce the frustration is to consider how familiar the person for whom you are selecting the Bible is with biblical language and theological concepts. In other words, how biblically literate is the person?

Many of the modern dynamic versions are designed to make the Bible accessible to persons whose English vocabulary is limited or who are unfamiliar with biblical imagery, cosmology, and rhetoric. Dynamic versions are often excellent starting points for people who need a more accessible Bible. However, if a person is well schooled in biblical literature and Christian traditions, dynamic translations can be jarring. Most people over 40 years of age are more familiar with the Bible and its stories and more comfortable with the concepts presented in traditional biblical language than younger people are. A dynamic translation may be stimulating for such people, but a more verbal version may serve their basic needs better.

Remember, there is no one set of correct answers to this question. Each person is different; the goal is to make sure that the Bible fits the individual.

How Will the Bible Be Used?

For much of its history the Bible was available only in one or two formats. Therefore, the same Bible was used for private reading and study, public worship, and devotional purposes. Today, however, we should think about versions of the Bible as we think about clothing. Most of us own more than one set of clothes. We wear certain clothes for playing and other clothes for working. Sometimes we dress up; other times we dress down. Some clothes are more versatile than others, and we can wear them in a number of different contexts. The same is true for Bibles, particularly in this era of specialization. Just as the Bible must fit the person for whom it is purchased, so also it must be appropriate for the use for which it is intended.

The first consideration is whether this Bible will be the only (or the main) Bible used. If so, it should be useful for reading (public and private) as well as for study. This broad range of uses would suggest one of the verbal translations, with the exception of the New American Standard Bible. One of the dynamic translations might be appropriate for this use, but the subjectivity of dynamic versions requires that considerable care be taken in choosing a dynamic translation for such a wide range of uses.

If this version will serve as one of multiple versions used, then questions about specific uses should be considered. For public reading and study the verbal translations will be more suitable. For private reading and study, particularly when combined with a verbal translation, the dynamic translations may be more helpful. Anyone who is intent on doing serious Bible study but is unfamiliar with the ancient languages should strongly consider using the New American Standard Bible or its updated version. This version is the only one firmly committed not only to a careful word-for-word translation but also to preserving the word order of the original texts. Although this philosophy makes the version difficult to read in public, it has no modern-language equal as a tool for private study.

While most people would prefer a verbal translation for public reading, if such reading will occur on a regular basis, care should also be taken to choose one of the verbal translations that pays careful attention to the rhythm and style of the English language.

What Format Fits Best?

Many people concentrate on this question before answering the more important questions mentioned above. In this era of intense competition for Bible sales, much of the energy of publishers has been spent in developing and marketing attractive formats. As a result many people are encouraged to choose a Bible for its format (binding, commentary or notes, translation helps, introductions, concordances, and the like), instead of for the usefulness of the translation.

Consider the question of format as a part of the process of choosing a translation. But ask it only after determining your answers to the first two questions above. Study Bibles and specialty Bibles will often be available in various translations. Choose a translation based on its merits and appropriateness rather than because it comes in the preferred format.

That is not to suggest that format questions are unimportant. Many of the notes, introductions, and other helps that are packaged in Bible formats enhance the usefulness of the translation. Often these additions are particularly useful because they are designed for specific situations and audiences. Some formats, such as a leather binding, for example, may lend a special air of sacredness to the Bible, reminding its reader that this book is not just another volume on the shelf. Other formats, such as hardback or paperback, may increase the reader's level of comfort, encouraging a deeper exploration of the text.

One note of caution needs to be sounded before we proceed further. Many publishers have combined the biblical text with the study or devotional notes of well-known clergy or authors. The result is a volume that takes advantage of the popularity and name recognition of the commentator to sell the Bible in a particular format. In study Bible or devotional formats, for which this is often done, such commentaries can be useful and informative, but they may also be biased or prone to errors of fact and interpretation. For this reason, these Bibles need to be carefully examined before they are selected.

After answering these questions you are ready to begin the process of choosing a translation. We offer the following suggestions to help you through that process.

Do Your Homework First

Selecting a Bible is an important choice. Unfortunately, most people devote considerably less time and effort to choosing a Bible than they should. We know people who spend weeks researching and comparing products before they buy anything, even a small appliance. They search through magazines, consult *Consumer Reports,* seek the advice of friends, and comparison shop before actually making a purchase. But most people spend less than thirty minutes choosing a Bible.

The process of choosing a resource as important as the Bible deserves more time and thought. Reading our book is a good start.

Learn about the differences between modern versions *before* you start asking questions of trusted friends or sales clerks.

Make an Informed Decision.

Having gathered your facts, put them to good use. Once you have determined which translation or translations suit your needs, stick to your choice. Notes and commentary are not the Bible itself, but publishers have discovered that people do not want to buy *just* a Bible. Consumers are interested in options, and so publishers make numerous ones available. Check which translation a Bible that attracts your eye is based on. Review its strengths and weaknesses by checking this guide or another similar book. Make certain both the translation and the format suit the reader of the Bible. It is likely that your favorite translation is available in your favorite format. If time allows, shop around to find the combination of translation, format, and price that you desire. Selecting a version before deciding on the format will ensure that your Bible will be a cherished part of your life for many years.

Using a Translation

As with any other book or tool, ownership is not enough. We buy books to read; we buy tools to use. Whether one chooses to look at the Bible as a book or a tool, having one (or a dozen) sitting on the bookshelf is no guarantee of success. Success depends on the choice of the proper tool that meets the challenge and enables the completion of the task.

Demands on our time and energy and changes in the world around us discourage us from engaging the Bible seriously. Early in this century most people would not only have been familiar with the Bible and its stories and teachings, they would have been living in a world permeated by the Bible, its language, and its ideas. The development of technology and the proliferation of information have forced the Bible to compete for a place in our culture. An explosion of literacy accompanied by an explosion of published literature has pushed the reading of the Bible into specific situations. Few of us read or study the Bible outside of a religious context, and the number of Christians who are willing to do even that continues to dwindle. Churches have spent the last half of this century fighting over the Bible or using the Bible to support their conflicting theological positions. In the process the Bible has lost its central place even within the walls of the church.

Reading the Bible has come to be a voluntary and intentional activity. Bible reading and spiritual exercise must be approached as diligently and intentionally as physical exercise. In a world full of distractions and barriers, we must make a conscious decision to develop the habit of reading and studying the Bible. An important part of making that decision involves understanding and trying to remove the barriers that prevent us from coming to the Bible.

Once you commit yourself to incorporating the Bible into your routines, consider carefully how you will use it. The truth of the Bible rests in its ability to transform the lives of its readers. But this can only happen when we immerse ourselves so completely in its pages that it becomes the very foundation from which we live out the faith. The Bible is full of wisdom, but the diversity of the texts it contains (i.e., the narrative and poetic nature of many passages) means that is does not always contain straightforward answers to our particular questions. As we read the stories of the Bible, we ask a simple question: How should I live in light of these stories?

To this end, we remember that Jesus cautioned his followers to be "wise as serpents and innocent as doves" (Matt 10:16, New Revised Standard Version). Approaching the Bible we seek to look deeply into the texts. You probably ought to have at least one Bible that has as few interpretative notes as possible. Reading this version would allow you to experience the text first before encountering commentary and explanation. In addition, take considerable care to evaluate the quality and theological biases of the notes that are a part of the format you are using. Finally, you ought also to consult notes and commentary from sources other than your study or devotional Bible. This will remind you that other ways of reading this particular passage also exist, and your understanding of the passage will be enriched by the comparison.

Beyond concerns about narrow interpretations in accompanying notes, it is also important to look across the breadth of Scripture as you study it. Many people are surprised to learn that the chapter and verse divisions with which many of us are so familiar were not part of the original text of the Bible. In fact, they are a relatively recent addition. Most scholars agree that the current divisions date from the sixteenth century. They were introduced to allow persons using different translations or versions to follow the reading from the same passage.

If the Bible is to become central to the Christian's life, then we must attempt to recover a reading of the texts that gives attention to their nature as sacred *literature*. Therefore, Paul's letters need to be read as letters, not just as numbered theological statements. The Gospels tell a story with a beginning, middle, and end; we need to read those stories in their entirety, not just piecemeal. Psalms need to be sung; poetry needs to be recited. We must recover a sense of the dramatic force of the biblical text in order that it be allowed to live and breathe life into its readers.

Much of the anxiety involved in choosing a version will disappear if you are willing and able to use more than one version, particularly in the context of study. The advantage the availability of so many versions gives is that we no longer must rely on just one translation and its interpretation of the ancient texts.

Therefore, we recommend that you use at least three versions. One should be a verbal translation; the other two could be dynamic translations, perhaps with different levels of fidelity to the words and order of the ancient Greek and Hebrew. The process of reading and comparing the translations in this way will enrich your understanding of the text and aid you in hearing nuances of meaning that may be obscured in the translation process. Should you be limited to one translation, however, we strongly suggest using a verbal translation with as little interpretative bias as possible.

An awareness of the differences between various translations will also remind you not to continue to search for the "right" or "best" version. The version that is right for you is the one that best serves your purpose at the point of use. Fight the urge to find the one version that will serve all your needs equally well. No serious mechanic would try to repair a complicated piece of machinery with only a pair of pliers. A full complement of tools is necessary for the successful completion of such a job. In the same way serious students of the Bible (and we believe that *all* Christians ought to be serious about their study of the Bible) need a broad range of tools at their disposal in order to read and understand the Scriptures that lie at the center of their lives.

Finally, as you read your Bible closely, you will quickly discover that the world of the Bible is hardly recognizable in our modern context. It is a world without modern technology and without mass communication. And the stories, written as they were for ancient audiences, have retained their ancient flavor.

Explanatory notes can help us visualize the modern equivalents of biblical events and locations, but the culture that pervades the world of the Bible must also be the subject of our attention. The Bible is an ancient document, set in an ancient culture. Some stories only come to life when one understands the contemporary Mediterranean culture. Others make sense only in light of the history of Israel, Egypt, and Greece. Most of the stories in the Bible will be confusing unless we have some knowledge of the geography of that world. Reading and understanding the Bible demand commitment to study, reflection, and prayer.

Conclusion

We hope that the information in these pages is useful, enlightening, and even inspiring. Choosing a Bible can be a wonderful journey of discovery. But take care to avoid the pitfalls. Remember that no single translation is the best or even the most correct among all of the modern English translations. But do not become so dazed by the range of choices that you are unable to choose.

In the end the decision is yours. The choice is not a final one, not in this era of new and newer versions. You will have a chance to choose again and again. Be sure to commit yourself not only to the choice of a Bible but to its use. Any book we affirm as Scripture ought to be read and used with joy and reverence.

After all, this book contains the words of the law of Moses, the writings of the prophets and holy ones of Israel, the stories of the life of Jesus, and the memories of his disciples. As so many have done before us, we commend them to you.

Abbreviations

ASV	American Standard Version
BCE	Before the Common Era
CE	Common Era
CEV	Contemporary English Version
ICB	International Children's Bible
JB	Jerusalem Bible
KJV	King James Version
KJ21	Twenty-first Century King James Version
LB	Living Bible
LXX	Septuagint
NAB	New American Bible
NASB	New American Standard Bible
NASB Update	New American Standard Bible, Updated
NCV	New Century Version
NEB	New English Bible
NET	New English Translation
NIV	New International Version
NIrV	New International Reader's Version
NJB	New Jerusalem Bible
NKJV	New King James Version
NLT	New Living Translation
NRSV	New Revised Standard Version
NT	New Testament
OT	Old Testament
REB	Revised English Bible
RSV	Revised Standard Version
RV	Revised Version
TEV	Today's English Version

Index of Contemporary Bible Versions